TESTIMON
MAXIMIZE YOUR SUCCESS

A must-read, packed with tremendous insight from the greatest, most successful network marketers in the world. Jordan Adler's approach and success in the industry and his network of superstars deliver once again!

Greg Hider
Rockstar Realtor
Phoenix, AZ

What's the difference between someone who does all right in network marketing and someone who is truly successful? Well, after reading this paradigm-shifting book, I am now convinced more than ever it is establishing a personal brand. And I am also convinced now that anybody can do it with the motivation and practical advice given in this book.

Warren Taryl
Taryl Accounting
Phoenix, AZ

Momentum Makers: Over 100 Tips From Network Marketers For Building Your Brand is packed with short, inspiring stories and eye-opening tips that can help you grow your network marketing business through branding awareness. Whether you're a veteran of the industry or brand new, you can learn new strategies and take immediate action from the stories and bullet points in each chapter to grow yourself and your organization. Plus I love how quick and EASY it is to read! I can share it with my team and know they'll actually read it! So simple and great for duplication in your organization.

Peter Kaufmann
Network Marketing Top Producer
New Orleans, LA

An amazing insight into how to level up in business through your personal brand and connect with your audience! This book really defines how success is a result of being authentically you!'

Hannah Geary
Wellness Digital Creator
Cambridge, England

Momentum Makers: Over 100 Tips From Network Marketers For Building Your Brand is the PERFECT book for network marketers! The authentic stories of real-life people make it easy to understand their struggles and triumphs, how they relate to our own experiences, and then teach us how to use them as a guide to push forward and ROCK IT in our own businesses. I wish I had this book when I first stepped into the network marketing world!

Melissa Calway-Barlock
Entrepreneur
Waterloo, Ontario, Canada

Momentum Makers: Over 100 Tips From Network Marketers For Building Your Brand is jam-packed with invaluable tips from the best of the best! A compilation of personal and applicable proven brand-building strategies from dynamic leaders.

Carla Falcone
Chief Marketing Officer, The Fearless Networker
Bend, OR

Have you ever picked up a book that you start reading and can't put it down? *Momentum Makers: Over 100 Tips From Network Marketers For Building Your Brand* is an amazing book that shows real stories of people's lives and what they have experienced in their own MLM journey.

Each of these 20 people clearly pointed out that branding is not about the company you may represent. It's about you!

I strongly urge you to take the time to read these amazing stories and learn and know that you can experience these incredible results.

Jim Carpenter
Network Marketer
Roosevelt, AZ

MOMENTUM MAKERS

Over 100 Tips From Network Marketers For Building Your Personal Brand

A Network Marketing Book By
Beach Money Publications

Published by Beach Money Publications
9885 Wyecliff Drive, Suite 200
Highlands Ranch, CO 80126
BeachMoneyPublications.com

Contributing Authors:
Angela McKay, Marina Simone, Callie Teegardin, Terri McClure, Jaclyn Stanley, Maria Cyza, Amy Hicks, Geraldine De Pablo, Camille Hammerich, Emily Roberts, Wendy Larson, Rachel Pekarek, Torsten Sedlmeier, Bethanny Crouse, Carollyn Mushro, Summer Meyer, Courtney Luper, Rikki James, Dr. Dana McGrady, Julie Burke

Manufactured in the United States of America.

ISBN: 978-1-62865-818-7

CONTENTS

MARINA WORRE

FOREWORD

When Jordan Adler asked me to write a few words about branding for this book, all I could think of was *How can I possibly sum up everything I want to say about branding in ONLY A FEW WORDS?????* There's so much I could share, but let me get right to the heart of it.

As a co-founder of one of the most recognized and trusted brands in the network marketing profession, I want you to understand that there is a great responsibility in building a brand. Yes, your brand should be about your passions and the things that are important to you but, in order to successfully grow your brand and leave a legacy, your brand needs to be built on a foundation that can become bigger than you.

People do business with people and brands they know, like, and trust. Once people get to know you and your brand, they will join you because they like you, they trust you, they connect with you, and they want—AND NEED—to be a part of something bigger than themselves. People will join you and your brand because they want to be part of a community and a winning team that wants to be and do more.

So, take the responsibility of building your brand seriously, but don't forget to have fun. Give yourself permission to:

- Be Bold
- Be Authentic
- Be Okay to Be Messy (while you're learning)

- Keep Improving
- Ask for Help
- Dream Outrageously Big!

Jordan has assembled an amazing collection of personal branding experts who are going to share with you exactly what you need to know and do to build a brand that has impact, staying power, and the ability to attract like-minded people to your business now and far into the future.

Just remember, all business is conversation. If no one is talking about your business, you don't have a business. "What" they are talking about is up to the brand you build. So, GET CLEAR . . . GET CREATIVE . . . and most importantly . . . GET STARTED!

Marina Worre

Co-Founder & CEO of *Network Marketing Pro, Inc.*

Co-Creator of *Go Pro Recruiting Mastery/Virtual Go Pro Event*

Creator of *The Most Powerful Women in Network Marketing Event*

Founder & CEO of *Worre Studios*

JORDAN ADLER

FOREWORD

The truth is, I have never read a book on branding. I have never pursued branding as a mission or intention. I have never even "Googled" it! Yet, I guess I have a worldwide brand that is recognizable. Beach Money is known around the globe. And when you see or hear Beach Money, it leaves you with a feeling. When you hear it, you visualize "Dreams." You feel "Freedom." It's palpable. Today, tens of thousands of people are hashtagging #beachmoney because it says something, and it means something. People want Beach Money.

Many years before ever making one penny in network marketing, I was trying little classified ads to get leads for my network marketing business. I had never signed up one person. My budget was thin. I could buy a 3-line ad for $150, and that was a stretch. Typically I would get 3-5 calls from a single 3-line ad. One time, I just thought of the phrase "Beach Money," and I used that as the heading to the ad, and I got 30 calls. That little headline gave me five times as many leads! And although I never had any success signing anyone up, I remembered that.

Many years later, after finding my groove and building a successful network business, I decided to write a book to document my journey. My intention for the book was for someone to read it and leave with the feeling, "I can do it. I can succeed at living my dreams." The problem was, I didn't have a title for the book. But then I remembered the results I got from that little ad and realized that it would make a great title for the book because it says it all! And it turned out to be the perfect title. When people heard what the book was called, they wanted to read it! Who doesn't want Beach Money?

But this all happened because I followed my intuition. It's hard to teach someone that. My brand has a story. My brand is clear. My brand describes me and what I'm about in life. But the truth is, I didn't design it intentionally. I just followed my passion and stayed true to who I am. And I was clear about what impact I wanted to have in the world.

The way I see it, your brand is the feeling others are left with when they think of you. What do they remember about you when they meet you or see you on social media? This is your brand.

We all have a brand, whether we are in business or not. People form opinions of us based on how we move through life. That opinion is representative of our brand. Think of five people that you know. In 1-3 words, describe them. This is their brand.

Here are some examples:

"Invisible"

"Out there"

"Smart"

"Thoughtful"

"A little crazy"

"Out of control"

"Trainwreck"

"Partier"

"Driven"

"Type A"

"Plays big"

"Dreamer"

"Family guy"

"Superwoman"

I don't see myself as an expert on building a brand, but I do have a successful one. I believe that the truer you stay to who you are, the stronger your brand will be. Because it is authentic. And it doesn't have to be what you think it should be. It needs to be who you are! Let's look at comedians who have a brand. Imagine Rodney Dangerfield. What if he believed he needed to be more professional? It would have messed up his brand. He was funny because he was being himself. "I don't get no respect. No respect!" Or Eddie Murphy . . . can you imagine if he had tried to mimic the style of another famous comedian? Wouldn't work. He needed to be HIM. You need to be you however you are! Even if it's not what you think others want from you. Some people are jerks. And some people have developed very strong personal brands being jerks! A jerk that acts like a nice guy won't be taken seriously.

The authors that have contributed to this book are experts. They all have a success story, and you can learn a lot from them.

As I was reading the chapters in the author's copy of this book, my first thought was, "There is no college course that will offer as much value on why it's important to have a brand and how to create it that is better than this book." You will get everything you need to create a powerful brand that will attract all the right people into your life and your business. I'm excited for you to read this book. It's the best resource for building a personal brand that I have ever come across. I'm excited to hear the stories you create after applying what you learn here.

ANGELA MCKAY

BUILDING A PERSONAL BRAND THAT WORKS FOR YOU

My network marketing journey found me in my laundry room. Yes, my laundry room . . . I know, you might be scratching your head and asking yourself, "Why the laundry room?"

Well, for starters, I am a busy mom raising seven amazing kids, which translates into A LOT of laundry and a pretty chaotic life, from cooking meals to art projects, cleaning the home and, you guessed it, A LOT of laundry. I wore many hats in my daily life as a mom. But there was one hat that was missing in my life.

It was a winter morning, and I was exhausted. I headed to the laundry room to start my busy day and remember just wanting a hot cup of coffee and a shower. I instead stood in my laundry room staring at the basket of missing socks. It wasn't the socks that made me start my ugly crying—although I dislike this chore—it was a reminder of how I truly felt like something was missing from my life as a woman, and that basket represented it.

I felt guilty because I loved being a mom, but I also loved the drive and fulfillment of being a businesswoman. I decided I wanted to do more for our family and, let's face it, that many diapers can add up.

An opportunity came and although it took me out of the home, I felt better knowing I was contributing to our family's future. I was determined to make my new retail store a success. I felt excited and determined, but as

I flipped the open sign, that mom guilt came flooding back. I had found what I thought was missing, but still had time debt and missed mom moments. I felt like I was right back where I started and suddenly it was the same tug of war in my heart for what was best.

I was on the hamster wheel of life. I felt exhausted from running a retail store and raising a family. That's when I believe network marketing found me by default of some much-needed mommy energy I fell in love with the products, however I was very firm that I had zero desire to sell anything . . . after all, I had a business and very little time. Two weeks later, I received a check in the mail from that same company, and I was confused. I had said I wanted nothing to do with the business so why in the world did they pay me?

It was the light bulb moment that changed everything.

I went home and shared this with my husband. I was still confused about why they paid me when I put in zero time, but I was curious. After all, time was more precious than income to a very tired mom. I couldn't stop thinking, "What if I tried to earn an income?" I knew I was a marketer, and I could sell anything if I believed in it.

Fast forward from that day in the laundry room to today. Both my husband and I have worked from home raising our seven children over the last decade. We have found not only the time to be work-from-home parents, but I also found what was missing in that laundry room that winter morning looking at a basket of missing socks: I found myself and my passion as a business coach. I love helping others build their network marketing businesses and having dinner as a family every night. I don't dread looking at the basket of missing socks anymore, and instead, they are intentionally a reminder of staying grounded in living your purpose in life. I believe you can have it all as a network marketer and I'm proof that it can work.

So how did I do it? I branded myself in my business.

"A brand is a voice and a product is the souvenir."
—Lisa Gansky

Welcome to your branding breakthrough! Yes, friend, I am excited for you because what you're about to learn will not only take your income to the next level but it will also take the stress out of building a business altogether.

I can assume that if you're reading this, you are in one of two places in your business: You are new and eager to learn how to build a personal brand to grow your income, or you are feeling frustrated and struggling with this entire idea of branding and are about to throw in the towel.

Let me tell you, friend, I have been in both places in my career and what I am going to share with you comes from the mistakes and lessons I have learned firsthand in my own business. As a networking marketing mom, I had a midlife brand crisis at forty years old. What I mean is that I found myself struggling with my own voice and professional identity and was doing it all wrong. I did what I saw others in the industry doing, and I branded myself as my company.

MISTAKE #1 – I AM NOT MY COMPANY'S BRAND

I was that girl on social media that looked like a product infomercial vomiting sales with every stroke of my keyboard. I call this my post and pray phase. It felt easy and my up line said, "Just do as I do and be consistent." After about 60 days of this, the only thing I was consistent at was getting frustrated at not getting results. Luckily I am not one to sit on the insanity of repeating mistakes, and I took it upon myself to learn the art of personal branding.

Looking back, I now see that I had no idea what a personal brand really was, and I just thought branding was a cool logo, colors, and slogan—you know, the pretty stuff. And although those are parts of the branding process, they are not what define a personal brand.

So what is a personal brand?

A personal brand is not logos, fonts, colors, or slogans. We know now it's not even your company. So what defines a personal brand? YOU . . . Yes, friend, you are your brand.

MISTAKE #2 – BUILDING YOUR PERSONAL BRAND SETS YOU APART

Many think the key to a personal brand is to grow an income, and although this is somewhat true, it is more than making money as an entrepreneur. I call these the pillars of your brand.

Pillar #1- You want to stand out in a crowd.

As a network marketer, we know that we are not the only person selling our products or recruiting a team in our company. So how do we stand out? We showcase our personality and interests so that we have connection points with potential clients using our personal brand.

I want you to write down 5 interests you have that make you who you are. Things other than your company—for example, mom, dog owner, traveler, baker, runner, gardener—things that you have an interest in outside of business. This list will play into our second pillar.

Pillar #2 – Building a personal brand grows your network.

Remember old me, the social media infomercial chic? Why do you think back then I struggled with results in my business? That's right, I was creating resistance with all the marketing posts, and no one could connect with me unless it was about business. When I got frustrated and started educating myself on personal branding and creating value, I started noticing something. When I used my list of interests and hobbies and created value-based content, I started having conversations. My audience that shared those same interests started commenting and messaging me. I started creating relationships, and out of curiosity, they started to ask me questions, including what it is that I do for a living. You see, adding value and creating curiosity is how I still use social media as a tool for my business. It allows me to not feel frustrated but instead be excited about showing up and sharing. People now know me for my Laundry Room Diaries Podcast and as the mom boss that shares hilarious mom life stories and business strategies to empower the modern-day mom boss. When I finally found myself in my brand, I also found my audience and ways to talk to them. This is key in business to continue to grow your network.

Pillar #3 – Nothing lasts forever.

In today's ever-changing world, businesses come and businesses go. It wasn't until I saw my former company switch from a MLM to affiliate, and I saw the network I had built for seven years disappear with it that I woke up. And although we hope our company lasts a lifetime, it would be pretty irresponsible to assume this and not take action to protect the time and money of our business investment. Your personal brand is like insurance in your business.

By using what we have learned about creating a connection point to an audience through your personal brand and not your company's brand, you have seen that a personal brand sets you apart from the crowd and attracts the buyers to you. Using key interests and personality lets your customers build trust with you, and in the unfortunate circumstance something happens or you simply decide to make a change, your audience goes with you because they are attached to your brand and not a company.

You now have a clear view of why building a personal brand is not only important but is key as a network marketer. With some clarity and consistency, you will start to see a less stressful way to build connections and grow your business. The best time to start a personal brand is when you decide to start your business. There is no need to wait until a certain goal is achieved. Start where you are and remember: YOU are what makes your brand unique and special. Take these pillars and apply them today and I cannot wait to see the impact it has on your business.

MOMENTUM MAKERS

1. **YOU ARE YOUR BRAND, NOT YOUR COMPANY.** A personal brand is not logos, fonts, colors, or slogans. We know now it's not even your company. So what defines a personal brand? YOU . . . YOU are the brand you should be promoting.
2. **START BUILDING YOUR BRAND WHEN YOU START YOUR BUSINESS.** The best time to start a personal brand is when you decide to start your business. There is no need to wait until a certain goal is achieved. Start where you are and remember: YOU are what makes your brand unique and special.
3. **BUILDING A PERSONAL BRAND IS THE INSURANCE ON YOUR BUSINESS FOR YOUR FUTURE.** By creating a connection point to an audience through your personal brand and not your company's brand, that personal brand sets you apart from the crowd and attracts the buyers to you.
4. **IDENTIFYING INTERESTS AND HOBBIES WILL ALLOW YOU TO CREATE CONNECTION POINTS TO HELP YOU FIND YOUR IDEAL CLIENTS.** Write down five interests you have that make you who you are and start sharing them on social media. Your audience that shares those same interests will start commenting and messaging you. Create relationships, and out of curiosity, they will start to ask you questions, including what it is that you do for a living.
5. **YOUR BRAND WILL GROW WITH YOU AS YOU GROW YOUR BUSINESS.** Building a personal brand is not only important but is key as a network marketer. With some clarity and consistency, you will start to see a less stressful way to build connections and grow your business.

MARINA SIMONE

YOU ARE YOUR BRAND

I missed my daughter take her first steps. That was a day I will NEVER forget. I was a single, broke mama who thought she had no choice but to work overtime just to keep the lights on.

I remember that exact moment. I was sitting at my cubicle, and my boss had just put a stack of more spreadsheets on my desk. I looked at the clock; it was 5:45, and I was again going to be late to pick up my daughter from day care.

Then I got a text from my friend at the day care center and it said, "Anaiyah just walked!"

In that moment I felt like a failure. What else was I going to miss in her life because I was strapped to a cubicle for someone else?

It wasn't until a year later when I was introduced to network marketing. All I heard was "make more money," and "fire your boss" and I was IN. It did, however, take my old friend from high school three months of follow up before I actually signed up.

I didn't have the money for the initial investment, so I had to find a way to make it work, borrowing the money I needed to finally get started. Was I scared? Yep. Was I afraid this was a scam? Sort of. But deep down I knew if I didn't change, nothing was going to change.

Here I am now almost 10 years later, and I had a full circle moment last month. I was able to watch my 10-month-old, Madelyn, take her first steps. WHY? Because I built a seven-figure income ONLINE from home by creating a personal brand that impacts other moms to go from the #cubcile2throne.

Let me introduce myself properly. My name is Marina Simone, and I teach moms how to slay online sales by identifying their brand, their message, and the impact they want to make by leveraging social media to build a network marketing empire.

Never in a million years did anyone in my city that knew me think that a broke, broken, hot-mess chick like me would be impacting an audience of over 100,000, building a seven-figure income from home, creating a team of 30,000+ being featured in magazines, speaking on stages, growing influencer brands, and becoming a top-12 income earner in her network marketing company.

Why?

Let me explain.

I was a party girl with no real vision. No mission. It wasn't until I was backed into a corner that I was FORCED to find a better way to provide for my daughter.

When I say I was broken:

I was sexually assaulted until I was 10 years old by someone in my family.

I was engaged to a leader of a gang who was physically abusive and committed murder in front of me.

I had a baby as a single mom.

I suffer from bipolar disorder and PTSD.

THE LIST GOES ON . . .

So how did someone like me, broken and with no future, become a top-income-earner in her company and build a seven-figure brand?

I didn't let my story define me. I took my story and flipped it from embarrassment and fear and took massive action to find ways to change my story and create new chapters of what I wanted my life to be like. Especially for my daughter.

I became a student of the industry.

I became a student of personal development.

I studied the leaders at the top—how they walked, dressed, and spoke and what their daily methods of operation were.

I copied the right cats until I found my own flow. My own DMO. My own voice. My real story. My brand.

I learned that my pain and my struggles were the start of impacting another human.

Maya Angelou said that people don't remember what you say but how you make them feel. I reminded myself every day before every presentation that I had an opportunity to make moms FEEL like they were worthy no matter what their story was.

It became my mission to impact moms everywhere—to empower them to let their stories be their true freedom into impact and profit.

But let's take a step back for a second.

Why and HOW do you build a personal brand without being an influencer first?

You probably see others leveraging brands on social media to sell products and attract leaders into their businesses, and you want the same, right? But how?

In 2012, *Forbes Magazine* talked about the POWER of building a brand. "Building brands builds value around companies."

People buy people, then they buy brands. Wouldn't you agree? Think of any product you buy over and over again. Someone had influence over you buying it. People buy WHY someone does something or uses a product.

Apple made history by becoming the first U.S. company to reach $1 trillion market value. Why did Apple do this better and, yet, how the hell? They stayed ahead of their competition, yes, but the #1 reason is they put their consumers, or tribe, of people first. They focus on values and value their consumers. The products they create solve a problem for their consumers. How else could they get people like me and you to spend $1000 on a cell phone every two years?

Most quit when it comes to building a personal brand on social media because the results are not overnight. To grow your circle of influence it takes time. While your friends are watching Netflix and chillin', you'll be collecting checks and chillin' all by building a SuperFan Personal Brand on social media.

Kylie Jenner

Kardashians

Justin Bieber

What do they have to do with branding?

Justin Bieber was found on Youtube.

Kardashians exploded with SnapChat.

And Kylie Jenner exploded her business with Instagram.

Ask yourself this: Have you ever purchased a brand or product because a celebrity sold it or promoted it? I am sure you have. This is called social influence. It is the hottest way to make a sale to a consumer's heart.

You know their story.

You've connected with them.

Now you want to support them or be like them.

This is the power of building a personal brand.

Social media has allowed us, non-influencers, non-celebrities, to use social influence to build a personal brand and tribe of humans who want to be impacted by our stories and buy our products.

You are probably scared right now to start sharing your story on social media.

Maybe you think you don't have one.

Here's the deal.

You have impact to make.

Your story is powerful.

If you think it's small, someone else will think it's big.

You chose this industry because you are a leader.

You chose this industry because you have a story.

You were called to this industry to make impact.

You are your brand.

Start sharing your story

Provide value and watch your influence grow.

MOMENTUM MAKERS

1. **YOU ARE YOUR BRAND.** Not your company you joined and not the product you sell.
2. **YOUR STORY DOES MATTER AND WILL IMPACT SOMEONE ELSE.** Someone needs to hear your story so start sharing it!
3. **YOUR VALUE IS NOT DEFINED BY THE # OF FOLLOWERS ON SOCIAL MEDIA.** Even if you impact ONE human you have won.
4. **SOCIAL MEDIA IS A TOOL TO REACH NEW LEADS THAT ARE LOOKING FOR WHAT YOU HAVE TO OFFER.** Lead with value and show up everyday to serve on social media.
5. **STOP WAITING TO START TELLING YOUR STORY.** The longer you wait to tell your story and share your message is the longer you stay stuck and keep showing up spammy on social media.

CALLIE TEEGARDIN

WHAT IS A PERSONAL BRAND?

Do you know what a personal brand is? Do you realize everyone has a personal brand? Do you know how to create one? (Neither did I until I started "to do things" and saw what "stuck.") Why is having a personal brand important? So many questions, let's dig in.

Your personal brand is *what we think of you,* and *what we think of you* is critical to your success. Why? Because we want to build relationships and do business with people we know, like and trust. We want to connect with you—the real, authentic and credible you. We want to know you care about us, more than you care about selling your product.

Your personal brand is what builds relationships and turns a sale into a long-term client or even friend. Here's the big question: Are you defining your personal brand? Or are you allowing others to define it for you?

Ready to take control of your personal brand, show the world who you are and attract people to your uniqueness? Great! Below are four critical "to-do things" I uncovered that led me to my successful personal brand. It took me over five years to figure this out—until I had an "a-ha" moment. Great news . . . it doesn't have to take you that long! With these four ideas you can be on your way to your own personal brand in an hour or two.

IDEA #1 – TOP 100 LIST

What's a *Top 100 List*? It's a list of items you want to accomplish during your lifetime. It will include business goals, fun goals, travel, different experiences, adventures and anything you really want to accomplish in your life. Why 100 items? Why not!? The bigger the list, the bigger the dreams.

Where do you start? With you! It's time to dream big!

- Who do you want to be?
- What do you love to do?
- What makes your heart sing?
- What would you like to accomplish personally and professionally?

Don't edit what comes to mind as you ask yourself these questions because your ideas/answers will feed your *Top 100 List*. Below are some life-changing goals/dreams I've accomplished from my list:

1: Promote to executive in my network marketing company

#12: Promote to senior executive in my network marketing company

#22: Read 50 books in one year

#55: Climb the Sydney Harbour Bridge

#60: Become a master scuba diver

#65: See the Egyptian Pyramids

#66: Scuba dive the Red Sea

#72: Write and publish a daily blog

#91: Take a 4-month trip

When I wrote my list, each item was just a dream/goal. When you write down your dreams and goals, amazing things can happen.

Turning Dreams into Action

After writing your *Top 100 List*:

1. Highlight the goals you want to accomplish in the next twelve months.
2. Narrow the highlighted list into three things you specifically want to focus on during the next twelve months.
3. Create a game plan around each of the three.
4. Create the daily activity to make it happen.

IDEA #2 - A DAY IN THE LIFE

Congrats, you just got in touch with your dreams, goals and desires. Now it's time to create a vision of what your life will look like in five to seven years, which is crucial because you're not static and neither is your personal brand. You are going to change and grow. Your brand needs to grow with you.

For example, in his book *Beach Money*, my friend Jordan Adler describes what beach money is and why you want it. He shares about a trip to Venice Beach that triggered his "Beach Money" lifestyle dream. This is key, because his "Beach Money" lifestyle became part of him and his brand *long before he had Beach Money*. **He grew into his brand because he knew where he wanted to go**.

It's time to write down your ideal *A Day in the Life* story just like you want it to look five to seven years from now. If you were to have both time freedom and money freedom, what would your life look like?

- Where would you live?
- Who would you spend time with?
- What does your life with your partner/spouse look like? What about with your family?
- Are you retired or still working?
- Do you have one income stream or multiple? How much do you make?
- What would your normal day look like?
- Where would you vacation?
- What do you do for fun?
- What on your *Top 100 List* are you pursuing?

I wrote my first *A Day in the Life* story in December 2016. At the time, I was divorced and single. The fourth paragraph begins, *"I'm sharing my life with an amazing man that totally gets me. He encourages me to be me and to continue on the growth path that I have been on for the past few years."* I go on and describe other things I am looking for in a partner and our relationship. Six months later I met Steve on a scuba diving trip in Egypt. We were married in December 2018. As I reflect back on the words I wrote, I find they describe my husband and our relationship in detail.

The funny thing is, I was only on that scuba diving trip because #65: See the Egyptian Pyramids and #66: Scuba Dive the Red Sea were on my *Top 100 List*. When the opportunity presented itself, my friends didn't want to go and my mom was nervous about me traveling to Egypt. I considered not going until I realized I didn't want to live my life saying, "I wish I would have." Instead, I said "yes" because it was part of my *Top 100 List*. Had these goals not been on my list, I may have never met and married Steve.

Knowing what you want in life is key. When you write it down and read it daily, you focus on your goals. What you focus on in life is what you create. Here's another example.

My *A Day in the Life* story begins with, *"It's a beautiful morning as I watch the waves roll in over the beach. In many ways my life is like a vacation because I get to choose how, when and where I work and play. As I look out at the ocean, I smile at all of the amazing things that have happened in my life. I love the freedom to travel and be able to live all over the world."*

Many mornings in the past three years I've awakened breathing the ocean air. I have been able to work and play on six different continents and several islands while traveling the world (including accomplishing #91 on my *Top 100 List*: Take a 4-month trip). It happened because I dreamed it; I wrote it down; and I focused on it daily by reading both my *Top 100 List* and my *A Day in the Life* story.

IDEA #3 – SOCIAL MEDIA STRATEGY

You've created your vision using your *Top 100 List* and by writing your *A Day in the Life* story. Time to live your vision and share it on social media. Using social media to build your personal brand requires consistency. I recommend starting with one platform. I prefer Facebook. It's been great for me; some of my team love LinkedIn, and others love Instagram. Which one is best for you?

Whichever resonates the most with you and your style, start there ***and get great at it before adding another platform.*** Trying to be all things to all people on every social media platform dilutes your audience. When you do expand to a second platform, spend 80% of your social media time on your first platform and 20% on your second.

So what is the *Social Media Strategy?* It's choosing three to five things that define who you are and what you are passionate about. How do you figure them out? Answer the following questions:

1. What's most important to you?
2. What do you want people to think of when they think about you?
3. What aspects of your life do you want to be known for?

Knowing these answers will help you determine your *Social Media Strategy*. If you post about anything and everything, you confuse your audience. In creating your personal brand, your goal is not to be all things to all people; your goal is to become clear about ***who you are*** and the tribe you want to attract.

As I dug into this exercise, the five areas that resonated with me were:

- Traveling the World
- Living & Inspiring Freedom
- Having Fun with Friends & Family
- Enjoying Wine & Food
- Spreading & Receiving Kindness

All five fit me and where I am going. Having my list makes it clear on what to post about and how to show up in my life.

As you build your list, make sure everything is authentically you. My girlfriend Melanie loves dogs, and they are part of her *Social Media Strategy*. I like dogs, though they aren't my thing. I don't post about dogs. I posted about my mom's dog, Izzie, when I visited my mom because it fit into my *Social Media Strategy* (having fun with friends & family). If it's part of your list, it's part of you. Post away! If not, stay away!

It's important to work with three to five areas. Why? Because fewer than three, you are very limited on what you can share. With more than five, you begin to dilute your audience and message.

You may have heard you shouldn't post about sports, politics or religion. If it's not part of your *Social Media Strategy,* then you definitely want to stay away. However, sports, politics or religion might be one of your three to five areas. If it's on your list, then post away and don't worry about who you might offend. You are not looking for that person. You are looking for your tribe and those who resonate with you.

A perfect example is my friend April. Her items include loving God/ loving Jesus. I admire and love this about her. She's authentic and stays in alignment with herself and how God and Jesus are working in her life. She attracts like-minded people to her. They are her tribe.

Please note, do not make the company you represent one of your items. None of the five on my list are my specific company. You are not your company. As humans we want to connect with other humans, not your company and not what you sell. Do I talk about my company and products? Yes, as it fits into one of my areas.

Every week I get a number of Facebook friend requests from people I don't know. When I go to their profiles to learn more about them, I don't want to connect if all I see is posts about their products and company. I see it across all professions. Have you been guilty of this? If so, it tells your audience nothing about you. You are missing out on attracting your tribe. People want to connect with you, the real, authentic you.

Should you share about your company and products? Yes, though only part of the time. Using the 80/20 rule is a good rule of thumb; post only 20% or less about your company and what you sell. Remember, the company you represent and what you do for a living are only a fraction of who you are.

Make your posts about your company and products creative, fun and intriguing. Remember, none of us want to be sold to, especially on social media. As soon as you put a call to action in your post (i.e. message me to learn more!!), most people will ignore your post because it feels like you are just trying to sell something. Instead create intrigue. Because when people are intrigued, they are more inclined to reach out or comment.

For example, let's say one of your areas is being healthy and your company has a healthy drink. You could take a photo of the drink with a fun background (your backyard) and post something like this:

It's time for my afternoon break and some fresh air. I love my Chai Tea. It's packed with all natural ingredients, helps soothe my anxious feelings, boosts my mood and keeps me from stress eating.

Ultimately, choose the three to five things that make the most sense for you. Not everyone on social media is going to resonate with you. That's okay. Be you. Be authentic. And. Just. Do. You. People want the real you, not you trying to be someone else.

IDEA #4 – CREATING YOUR PERSONAL BRAND

Once you define who you are and the areas to share, you are well on your way to creating your personal brand. It's okay if you don't know exactly what your personal brand is right now. It will emerge. It will emerge as you live and design your life.

My personal brand of *Finding Joy in the Journey* emerged from acting on a prompting. What's a prompting? It's your inner voice nudging you to take action. It was November 2017, and I was ready to head off on a sixteen-day trip.

Nine days before leaving, my mom unexpectedly passed away from a heart attack. It shook me to my core. I had always been told the 40s are the best years of your life. And in a matter of three years since turning the age of 40, I had gone through a divorce and lost both parents.

I contemplated canceling my trip, though I knew my mom would not be happy with that decision. She would have wanted me to continue living my life. She and my dad did not raise me to sit back and watch life; instead, they would have wanted me to fully participate in every moment. So I made a promise.

I promised my parents to find joy in the journey everyday on my sixteen-day trip. I also promised to share my experience with others. I knew if I had to share it, it would hold me accountable to stop and *find my joy in every day*.

My journey into my personal brand began with this commitment and a post on Facebook . . .

And I'm off . . . the 16-day adventure begins. The timing of this trip is interesting, so I'm naming it "Finding Joy in the Journey." I'll be doing one dedicated post each day. Since I typically post more than once a day, you'll find it as a black and white photo. I'll share the joy of the journey (on the trip or through this season), where I'm finding it and what I'm learning. I hope to inspire myself along the way. And if I can inspire others too, that would be a gift. So let the journey begin . . .

I always wanted to write a daily blog, but just the thought overwhelmed me. I didn't know how to get started. I even had it listed as #72 on my *Top 100 List*: to write and publish a daily blog.

When I acted on this "little" idea to share my 16-day journey while grieving, I had no idea that more than three years later I would **still be writing**. Oh, I've tried to stop. But every time I do, I get a message from someone telling me how my *Finding Joy in the Journey* daily post has made a difference in his or her life. How do you stop sharing when your mission in life is to inspire freedom and mentor people to find and live their great life?

Taking the time to write my *Top 100 List*, create my vision through my *A Day in the Life* story and hone in on my *Social Media Strategy* taught me to focus on doing things I love every day. Doing what I love (rather than just thinking about it or being busy all day) and sharing it on social media allowed my inner voice to lead me to my personal brand.

When creating your personal brand ***listen*** when you get a nudge or an idea to try something. Take Action. Try it! If it gets great feedback, continue to do it and play with it until you own it. My daily post has given me a platform to share me, to be vulnerable and communicate my story to the world. Your idea may be in video format, a blog or through pictures. The critical piece is when you find what works continue to do it. A brand doesn't build overnight; you have to be consistent over time.

I number each of my *Finding Joy in the Journey* posts. I am over 1,200 days of sharing. The numbering keeps me going, and it's a great strategy to implement; it shows your audience your commitment.

Your following may start small. Please don't compare your beginning with someone else's midpoint. We all start at the beginning. It takes time to build your personal brand and your following. Make it unique. Make it you. And be accountable to someone. Fortune has a way of smiling on those who follow through!

It's your time. Get started now and share your message with the world, because the world needs you!

MOMENTUM MAKERS

1. **CREATE A TOP 100 LIST.** Your TOP 100 LIST is a list of items you want to accomplish during your lifetime—it includes business goals, fun goals, travel, different experiences, adventures and anything you really want to accomplish in your life. The bigger the list, the bigger the dreams.

2. **CREATE A VISION OF WHAT YOUR LIFE WILL LOOK LIKE IN FIVE TO SEVEN YEARS.** This is crucial because you're not static and neither is your personal brand. You are going to change and grow. Your brand needs to grow with you.

3. **KNOW WHAT YOU WANT IN LIFE—THIS IS KEY.** When you write it down and read it daily, you focus on your goals. What you focus on in life is what you create.

4. **CREATE A SOCIAL MEDIA STRATEGY.** Live your vision and share it on social media, starting with one platform. Choose three to five things that define who you are and what you are passionate about. Using the 80/20 rule, post 80% about those things and post only 20% or less about your company and what you sell.

5. **WHEN CREATING YOUR PERSONAL BRAND *LISTEN* WHEN YOU GET A NUDGE OR AN IDEA TO TRY SOMETHING.** Take Action. If it gets great feedback, continue to do it and play with it until you own it.

TERRI MCCLURE

LEGACY IS EVERYTHING

Would you follow us if you never saw our eyes?

Would you listen to us if you never heard our voices?

Would you lead with us if you never saw our leadership?

To be in the business of network marketing you need to be seen. You need to have a voice, and you need to own your name. Who are you?

I proudly tell the world my name—I am Terri McClure, and I am joined in our networking business with my partner, Sam Long—two women who are constantly pushing boundaries and making statements on all levels.

For every Ying there is a Yang, and my Yang came in the form of a geophysicist. Sam simply fell in love. Sam saw the struggles in the business and decided to do everything in her power to help us achieve our goals. She resigned from her position and came to work. Sam saw my passion and my strengths, but more importantly she also saw my weaknesses.

Together we formed a partnership and our business began to flourish. First we needed to grow internally. We had no idea what we were doing and no clue as to protocols or what would be required to lead a successful team. Our love affair blossomed, and the business became our drive. We complimented each other beautifully. I was lousy at systems, but that was Sam's expertise. I was great at motivation, and Sam was straight down the line. We had every base covered, and we could see a vision for the future.

However, neither of us saw the expansive picture of what we can visualize today. We were simple people, earning enough to cover our bills, hoping that we would have enough money left over to celebrate with friends and meet our family's needs.

We realized that networking was simply a way to build relationships, and we found it hard to believe that people actually paid us money to have mates. Network marketing, after all, is just a room full of mates all chasing the same goal.

Together we created a brand that stands today as a household name in many families and countries around the world. We created an umbrella over our business to keep us protected. This umbrella allowed us to advertise in small groups without mentioning the parent company and to keep the integrity of the brand. This brand gave the team a sense of pride and a place to belong. It was the beginning of our family culture.

Each one teaches one is the philosophy of Mandela, and we used this principle to share our knowledge about health and business. We had a brand and now we needed customers. In theory, from the customers should become your social marketers.

We found traction on Facebook and became experts in attraction marketing. We set up groups for customers to share ideas and a place where they would be able to tell their stories in a safe environment. Today, in that same group, we have over 440,000 people, all sharing the same language. This became our amazing hub of customers, and from here people became our business partners.

The "how could I do this business?" question came without searching, and interest was created with people seeing success. We had built a strong customer base and had no real understanding of why we needed to build a team. Can you believe we even rang the parent company and asked the question "Do we need to do this? Why can't we just have customers?"

Residual income was the answer. Don't you want to go on holidays at some point and not worry? We had never thought about residual income and understood it was only for those people well above us in our tree, never understanding how the compensation worked and the value of eight deep.

We had to learn it did not matter when you joined a company. What matters is how fast you build your business. Are you going to take it on seriously? Are you going to fake work or are you going to see this as a valuable opportunity?

We set to the tasks of building systems for duplication and started talking like we knew it all. We were learning on the run and made loads of mistakes, upsetting people everywhere, but we were on a mission and were starting to gather momentum.

Our target avatar for our business was low socio-economic, having a belief that health should be affordable to everyone. From a business perspective we were looking for people who needed to create change in their lives. We had found a tool to make money, and all we had to do was teach what we had learned. We did not have a lot of money between us, so it was easy to work within our own networks. Poor people accumulate poor people. We were poor so it was easy to start with our friends.

Using the horse community as the base and starting in a small community in Western Australia, the network began to spread. We would travel miles talking to people and showing our faces. We began flying on planes with little money, just so that people would feel connected to the movement, to trust the vision and begin to talk about our culture that was multiplying.

Sam had created systems, manuals, and language for others to follow. Everything had been broken down to basics so that the new social marketer could understand how to build a business from the very beginning.

We learned to listen and share knowledge amongst our own leaders and look for easier ways to build. Empowering others was a whole new lesson. You cannot build a massive team alone, and you need support and leadership for everyone to feel valued. Leaders that are growing need to understand responsibility and how to enlighten others.

When we shared knowledge and educated the team to share points across lines to achieve titles, we gained movement and the team began to build with one vision. "Success loves speed" was something that we had been taught early in our career, and it was something we never forgot. Once we had momentum, we never stopped for anything. We were married in between titles, and we honeymooned after the job was done. We had a belief that this was going to be a business for everyone.

No one goes up the ladder alone, and no one achieves a title without a team; it is important for everyone to realize and understand their value. Personally, we love this about network marketing and the way the compensation plan is written. It keeps you humble and understanding that being a superstar alone is an impossibility.

The most important asset to any business is it creates culture. Because of our diverse relationship, Sam and I had this covered. Sam believed that all she wanted from this business was new mates. She did not care what color, creed, religion, or gender, there was going to be a home for everyone in the family that we were creating. I had visions of changing the world through the systems that we created and allowing women and now men to be able to make a difference in their lives. "Health, Wealth, and Choice" stands today as our mantra. People can now choose the life they want to live, whether it is to feed their kids or change their environments. The choices are now theirs to make.

Sam and I have thirteen legs, and within these legs we have transparency. Under our umbrella comes one huge family in which everyone knows everybody, and we communicate as one. We have built trust amongst us and are guided by solid policies and procedures to keep everyone's business safe. Leaders have become friends, and relationships have been formed no matter from which leg your business arose. We constantly do Zooms, and one of the most successful platforms we operate today is Power Hour in which everyone gets up at 5:45 AM and goes to work together. This one act is breeding huge success and propulsion.

Understanding how the compensation plan worked was an important part of our growth. If you are new in the industry our best advice would be to not bog yourself down in the details—simply understand how to make your first check then see what you need to make your second. The money will come if you do not over-complicate your thinking. Let your up-line guide you and get serious about the gift you have in your hands. Go to work. Set a fire in your gut that shines so brightly that nothing will destroy your reason for starting.

Titles and rewards will come with a successful team—we had to learn how to be humble. That sounds arrogant to say, but we really had no idea of the protocols of the business we had joined. They were strong lessons to learn, and today we guide others through what we learned from our mistakes. You always must remember where you come from and how you are perceived by your peers. At the end of the day it is a competitive industry that can love you or destroy you.

Education is vital for your business structure. Today we have "preschool" where new social marketers begin learning the business model—how we build and how we duplicate. They also learn the structure of the parent company and how we work together to form a partnership. We bring in other big leaders from other companies to tell stories, and we follow Frazer Brookes for his principles. Do not over confuse your teams with too many voices because the last thing you need is distraction. From "preschool" they graduate into the Big School, which runs four days a week, and everyone is expected to attend. Our leaders teach on the understanding that everyone is valued, and everyone has something to offer.

This is now a massive business behind the scenes, and we have hundreds of people who operate our systems in the background who are fondly named wizards, fairies, hobbits, and tigers. They give hours of their time to build and maintain the structure. It is certainly unique to network marketing, but it works and has created a safe platform for everyone to work without the fear of their customers being stolen. Trust is imperative when your team begins to grow and new blood arrives.

Today Sam and I operate our business from two hugely different platforms. I spend my time leading the team with the vision and the strategies for growth, and Sam is the Director of Operations, keeping the business safe and within the guidelines of TGA and Policies and Procedures.

We have been working hard to open new countries and to extend our growth outside of Australia. I am excited for this extension because it allows other cultures to be included within the business frame, adding a unique flavour to our family unit and teaching everyone compassion and an understanding of different cultures, language difficulties, and patience.

As the leaders, we look at the business today and are super proud of the different nationalities that we have incorporated into our family. We have always said there is a home for everyone, no matter if you are rich or poor, coloured skin or white, educated or not, there is a home for you here. We will educate, we will share, and we will bring you into our nucleus.

We have found our legacy; we have found our voices, and we have found why we are on this earth. The universe collided when Sam and I met. Everything happens for a reason.

We intend to leave a legacy for our children and our children's children.

Network marketing is an amazing tool if used correctly; use it to empower others to have self-belief, to change their lives, and to believe that they are good enough in this world.

Remember it is the simplest of words that can make a difference to someone else's world. Show someone you care, be grateful for their trust and lead the way. Never be mistaken, people are watching your every move.

Sam and I are grateful for our business and we are always humbled to share our story. Everyone has a story, but it is your task to make your story the best story for you.

I was 56 when I started this business, but it is never about how old you are or when you start. Instead, is about how hungry you are to succeed.

Find the superstar you have inside of you and let the world see your face. You are worthy of your success.

MOMENTUM MAKERS

1. **OWN YOUR NAME.** Not only on everything that you do on Facebook and Instagram, do not be scared to use your name. Use your name for every opportunity of profiling.
2. **ENCOURAGE YOUR NEW SOCIAL MARKETERS.** Understand who they are. Give them the strength to do the exercise "I am . . ." (ie. "I am humble . . .", "I am a mum . . .") Understand who they are.
3. **GIVE YOUR SOCIAL MARKETERS AN IDENTITY.** What makes them different?
4. **TEACH THEM TO HAVE COURAGE.** Have the courage to do a live, write a post, to speak, to have courage.
5. **RECRUITMENT.** Recruitment is key to all growth. Do not be scared to own the vision of your business.

JACLYN STANLEY

HOW TO BUILD A BRAND THAT IS AUTHENTICALLY YOU!

My name is Jaclyn Stanley. I'm a mom of three young children, and I've been married to my husband, Damien, for 10 years. I've been in the network marketing industry for a little over eight years. In my first few years, I definitely saw the potential in this industry and dipped my toes in with a company that was just not meant to be my permanent home. After that initial experience, I felt like I wasn't cut out for this type of gig because I had never recruited a single business builder and spent more than I made—not exactly my idea of a successful entrepreneur. However, I'm forever grateful for my time there because it opened my eyes to the possibility of network marketing as a legitimate career path.

Fast forward a few years to when I started what I call my "accidental successful business"—I was a new (reluctant) stay-at-home mom looking for purpose and community after having been a middle school social studies teacher and volleyball and track coach for nine years. I thought I knew all there was to know about network marketing, so I was not about to join my persistent friend who insisted I could be successful. So what did I decide to do? After ignoring her for at least six months, I ended up going all in and hit the top rank of my company in 15 months! It's funny how things work out, isn't it? While that fast ascent was super fun, it also came with its fair share of challenges. For one, I had to play catch up on all things personal development, including leadership, mindset, systems, and branding, to name a few.

Branding is a concept I didn't grasp right away, never quite finding the right book or podcast to help me along the way—the training opportunities on this topic just weren't what they are now. As I write this chapter, it's been a fun process to revisit what steps and missteps I took in order to learn the ropes, and it's also important to note that this is much like leadership in that you are always growing, adapting, and learning as you go.

I know you've heard it over and over again . . . "You need to determine your personal brand!" If you're like me, you may feel like this task is incredibly daunting, but what I eventually found was that avoiding this made my work more difficult. When you are clear on your brand, you will have an easier time developing content that catches people's attention and building your business in an authentic way.

One thing to keep in mind is that this personal brand will be a reflection of YOU—your values, your goals, and your motivation. You should never try to be someone else. If your brand isn't authentic to who you truly are, then it will be a total flop. The good news is that the process through which you identify your brand isn't as hard as you may think, and it can be a great way to get in tune with yourself.

So how do you establish an authentic personal brand that is simple to understand and likely to be respected?

Before we dive into that, let me share a story of branding gone bad featuring: me! I once thought that branding/attraction marketing was basically the same thing as bragging. I've never been a materialistic, designer-brand kinda gal. I have my splurges, but that's not my authentic self. I'm embarrassed to admit that I once did a Facebook live sitting on my bed surrounded by all of the big checks, gifts, prizes, etc. I had earned from my company. One by one, I held up items such as a Rolex, an invitation to Hawaii . . . All. The. Things. I went on and on about how awesome my company was, how awesome I was, how awesome all of these things were. *cringe* I think back to that video and want to hide. Can you imagine what my audience was thinking? Gag! The worst part is that I was totally not being myself. I was trying to be this fancy, super "extra" person that is not who I am. Much of what I put on social media at that time fell along these same lines. People who know me well were likely very confused, and those that didn't know me well certainly saw through that phoniness. Here's the thing: so many of us assume that we need to put ourselves out there in a way that others want or expect to see us when in reality, they just want to see the real, true you.

So what do you say? Why don't we dive right in and get to work!?

First up, you need to **get clear on your values**, which is so important because if you don't know what you care about, how can you properly communicate this with your audience? I've got a simple exercise that you can do to help guide you in this process. First, write down 10 of the most important values to you (things like leadership, integrity, honesty, service, creativity). Then ask yourself, "What would be devastating if people didn't think this was true about me?" That simple question should help you narrow your list down to three or four values. From there you can work toward adopting a saying that fits your core values. You could say something like "Influencing others to grow their income to make a greater impact" or "Influence + Income + Impact," which would encompass: influence, achievement, and service. Whatever statement you can boil your values down to is going to help guide every decision you make. The majority of what you put on social media should reflect your saying/values. Influence + Income + Impact is what I focus on when I share on social media, and I've found one of the most important ingredients in this recipe is authenticity. Can you see how the story I shared above does NOT reflect my values? One of the things that I've found to be effective is when I am vulnerable. One time I shared a "before" picture that was five years into my health journey. It was hard to post, but my "after" picture and the way people were able to relate with me was worth holding my breath as I hit the "post" button.

Another thing that can be super helpful when establishing your brand is to **find your uniqueness and exploit it for the service of others**. Social media is such a wonderful platform for network marketers to share what they have to offer, but this has also allowed the digital space to become flooded with new companies popping up every day. Because of this, you need to break free from the noise. Separate yourself from a crowded marketplace and stand out as the unique individual that you are. I once heard someone say something on a podcast that really stuck with me: "Different is better than better!" Consider these questions when searching for what makes you unique:

1. What problem do I solve?
2. What am I passionate about?
3. What could I give a speech about without much preparation?
4. What do I research?
5. What do I have results in?

I really love that last one for those of you who are veterans in this industry because the person you're positioned to best serve is the person you once were. Isn't that cool? I was that new stay-at-home mom looking for something outside of wiping runny noses and making peanut butter and jelly sandwiches. I feel that adrenaline rush when I meet someone in that similar situation because I know I can help them!

Next, you'll want to **schedule a recurring meeting with someone very important—YOU**! It is vital for us to regularly practice self-reflection so that we can ensure we are in alignment with our brand. We need to make time regularly to sit and reflect. Ideally, this will happen once a month, but at the very least you will want to schedule this quarterly. I suggest purchasing a journal to record answers to a set of questions that feel important to you. These questions may include:

1. What are my current goals?
2. What am I doing to reach these goals?
3. What have I been avoiding out of fear?
4. What risk can I take even in the face of fear?
5. What skills or talents am I not utilizing?
6. What does my business want that I'm not currently providing it?
7. What am I committed to changing?
8. How is my business communicating my values?

I love looking back on my journals to see how far I've come during these self-reflection meetings. Regularly assessing your goals and values through self-reflection can really help you evaluate your performance when you connect your business numbers (recruiting, sales, retention, etc.) to the work you put into your brand. Be sure that you are not squeezing this in between meetings or scheduling it at a time of day when you're exhausted. You want to be fully focused and committed to this meeting. I've gone through seasons in which I've attempted to avoid this at all costs. I wasn't proud of where I was and didn't want to look in the mirror to admit my faults. I've come to learn that it doesn't have to be this way. You can be honest with yourself AND give yourself grace simultaneously. I make sure to celebrate my wins during these meetings because this "words of affirmation" girl benefits even when the praise is coming from myself!

Another way to help develop your personal brand is to **create your very own advisory board**, which is a fancy way of saying that you should find people who have brands that you admire and write them down on a list. You want to look for people who display similar values and have characteristics that you admire. If these people are local, ask them out for coffee or lunch. If they aren't in your area or happen to be somewhat famous, simply follow them on social media and take notes on the way they present themselves—their habits and the type of content they post. These mentors can show you what is possible because they've paved the way. They can also reassure us that we are headed down the correct path. I also find that they motivate me to up my goals and perfect my brand.

My advisory board changes from time to time as my brand evolves or if I feel that our values no longer line up. One mentor, in particular, has really helped me up my game with social media. I've followed this seasoned network marketer for some time and have always been drawn to her energy. Her social media accounts have inspired posts and stories for my personal feed as well as what I share with my team. She's been a permanent member of the board . . . I should probably make her president!

Now let's talk about what you should actually post. One of the most successful ways to promote your brand, products, services, and opportunity is to **focus on storytelling**. People want to know how this product or opportunity has helped you. I know you've heard the saying, "People don't buy what you sell, they buy WHY you sell it." People are emotional buyers, and stories are the most effective way to reach them. This is why I asked you to get clear on your values because they will come into play when you share about both your products and opportunity. You want to paint a picture about how something will make them feel. One of my dear friends and teammates shared a raw and vulnerable story of how her family had filed for bankruptcy. She shared how it felt and what it looked like for her family before she experienced this opportunity and after. While this may have felt embarrassing at first, I can tell you that her audience found aspects of her story they could relate to and could see how this opportunity could enhance their lives.

I always say that if I can be successful in network marketing anyone can! While branding doesn't come naturally to most people (it certainly didn't for me), it can easily be learned. I've come to appreciate the journey of learning more about myself through developing my brand. As with all aspects of this business, branding is a continual learning process in which you can choose to find joy.

MOMENTUM MAKERS

1. **GET CLEAR ON YOUR VALUES.** Your message needs to be easy to communicate to others and even easier to understand. This can be accomplished by getting clear on what matters most to you.
2. **FIND YOUR UNIQUENESS.** Social media is noisy right now. The thing that can best help you stand out is YOU!
3. **SCHEDULE SELF-REFLECTION TIME.** Put it on the calendar in pen. This meeting is vital to your growth and development not only in your branding but in your business as a whole.
4. **CREATE YOUR ADVISORY BOARD.** Role models can be the perfect inspiration to create the perfect brand. The trick is to learn from them, not copy them.
5. **FOCUS ON STORYTELLING.** People want to know how your product or service will impact their lives. Facts are great, but people buy because of emotion.

MARIA CYZA

YOU ARE ALREADY THE BRAND

What does it mean to brand yourself?

It doesn't seem organic or authentic, does it?

Well, that is because it's uncommon for human beings to be "branded."

But what if I told you that YOU are the brand when it comes to your business?

Yes, you.

What!?

Allow me to share a little bit about my story, the road to branding and beyond.

I was born in 1973 in Brooklyn, NY. Funny growing up Greek in the heart of Bensonhurst, Brooklyn because eighty percent of our neighborhood was full-blooded Italian, and I loved every minute of it! I lived there until I was 23, and I say to this day that you can take the girl out of Brooklyn, but you can't take the Brooklyn out of the girl!

I have always been outspoken and gregarious—able to fit in with every crowd and not scared or nervous to speak out loud, even in moments when my voice shook.

I grew up in a talented family. My father, Michael, was a self-taught singer and Bouzouki player. He had a very successful business for over

35 years. He was a showman who never gave up when times were tough and business was a bit slow, always hustling and showing my brothers and me that we serve others no matter what. In everything we do, the people come first—their happiness, joy, and satisfaction are number one. He took pride in everything he did, and I watched every move. I started singing professionally at the age of 13. I mean, I sang at the age of 5, imitating the pop stars back in the 70s and 80s. My dad knew I had a talent, and he always supported my entrepreneurial spirit. My dad was my hero. Even though he is no longer here with us, he lives within me through every move I make. His hand on my shoulder, whispering in my ear "Go, do this! DO NOT STOP. No matter what blocks, you will overcome them. You are a fighter and cut from a strong cloth."

My mother, Afrodite, was a 9-to-5 businesswoman and did everything to make our lives amazing. She went to college and took 12 credits and worked full time at a large commercial bank, and she was and is my role model, the absolute epitome of strength, kindness, and selflessness that I have ever seen in a human being. My mom showed me how to be strong over and over again. Many times she was going through so much and still looked to nurture and help others, never thinking about herself. I used to argue with her to do something nice for herself, but she filled her heart with helping and serving others. She is simply incredible, not because she is my mother but because God broke the mold when he created her.

So you see, I was set up to win from a child. Of course, I was a pain in the ass and broke rules and drove my parents crazy, but all in all, I was a good kid.

I didn't have an interest in school beyond high school. I just wanted to hustle and work. My parents weren't too happy about that, but I did it my way—the hard way. I have tried so many types of jobs from banking to make-up artist. I love to work, and I also love money. I take pride in working and being paid my worth as everyone should. In 1996 I moved to Bellaire, Florida, following my parents' retirement, and fell in love with the weather and my husband, Lenny. In 2000 we married, and in 2001 we had our beautiful, talented, and amazing daughter, Gabriella. We now live in Tampa, Florida, and are happy living near the Gulf of Mexico and enjoying our lives.

So how did I end up in network marketing?

In 2014 I was a relationship banker at a large commercial bank. It was closing time and two men decided to "stop by" and hold us up. I'm not going to go into the scary details, but let's just say in those couple of moments my entire life flashed in front of me and I was traumatized to my core.

I went from an independent woman to a scared, paranoid, emotionally scarred little girl when this ordeal took me back to other traumas I endured as a child and as a 14-year-old. I was sad, depressed, and afraid, and I don't know what I would have done with my life if I didn't have my husband, daughter, and family around to help me.

One afternoon after the robbery I was on Facebook and saw that a friend was having a "Facebook Party" for a cosmetic beauty company. I was invited and I bought a few products to try. I liked the stuff, so I was introduced to the idea of direct sales. I knew what direct sales was but never participated in the industry. Well, it was $99 to join and I hadn't gone anywhere and spent any money on myself, so my husband encouraged me to go for it, thinking it would help me get out of my shell and live life a bit better. I mean, in all fairness he was suffering, too, because I wasn't the Maria he fell in love with, and he was so worried about me.

I joined the company, and the first year was okay but nothing to brag about. I sold some things and built a small team, and my commissions were from $65 to $225 a month. The interaction was what I loved the most. But after that year I truly needed and wanted more—more of everything! I was getting back to my old self, and it felt great! I set big goals and wanted to be a six-figure earner at minimum. I wanted to shake the industry and really stand out, but I didn't know how. I had talents. I wasn't scared to talk to people or open conversations. I mean, if you were within three feet of me, I was going to let you know that I sold cosmetics and skincare and that "If you have skin, you need this." The next year I was with the same company and was invited to an industry event in Las Vegas that was to empower women in network marketing. There I was, sitting among them, six-, seven-, and eight-figure earners. And I felt like I truly belonged. My income didn't but my spirit did, and my energy was so high I felt like I could have floated out of that room. When the first speaker came out and told her story, that was it. I made the decision to continue and hit the ground running hard and fast toward my dream. NO MATTER WHAT. With my dad's hand on my shoulder and his whisper in my ear, I took the bull by the horns.

I knew that I had to stand out I had to be ME and no one else. I had to show up differently and be better than I have ever been, to work harder and smarter and put in the hours to develop myself in leadership, sales, product knowledge, and all aspects of the Direct Sales industry. All that was the easy part: read books, take notes, go to seminars, invest in coaching and mentoring, and implement the information to succeed. But that wasn't any different than anyone else doing what I was doing. I mean, everyone in that auditorium in Las Vegas was doing exactly that. I had to be different. I "hired" an assistant (myself, as a character) to work within my social media platforms to help me get product out there in front of people. She worked Facebook, Instagram, YouTube, and Periscope at the time—you name it, she was on it! Her name was Angie Castellano, and she was basically my help to sell more products. She did a video tutorial on how to put on makeup and people fell in love with her! She was funny, exciting, loud and crazy! She was a bit older than me (she was 65), and she took the direct sales industry by storm. Her videos went viral instantly with millions of views, likes, followers, shares, and more. Her videos were being recognized by cosmetic industry greats, and the *Huffington Post* wrote about her being a legend in her own time. She went on to do interviews and speaking engagements. She even went to Hollywood and worked with producers to pilot her own show. Angie was simply an idea that I had, and it took off in a very big way.

You see, I took my talent of making people laugh, mimicking voices, and doing different characters and brought it to life, a big chance for me. It had zero to do with makeup and nothing to do with sales, and it could have broken my entire career. The next thing I knew I was on a company incentive trip and lines were forming one hundred people deep to take a picture with me. People were walking up to me shaking, crying, and asking if they could give me a hug, sharing about how Angie changed their lives, helped them get out of depression, encouraged them to start a business, to not give up, and keep going stronger. It was a surreal experience that continued for years to come. Even to this day, people are starstruck when they meet me. I never understood that because I am Maria Cyza, a woman who has the same opportunity as everyone else in this world, not special or extraordinary. I simply needed to stand out. I had no idea this larger-than-life character would do just that for me and so many people worldwide. It was a humbling experience, and the most pivotal moment was when one of my customers called me to say her terminally ill little boy added meeting Angie to his Make A Wish. I will never forget that moment as long as I live. I still get emotional thinking of that call years later. The Character, my alter ego, Angie Castellano, lives today in my heart and often comes out to discuss makeup, world news, rigatoni and meatball recipes, and the love of her life, Sal.

The following years after Angie's debut were insane—huge sales, lots of sponsoring, and building my business. After I moved on to another company, Angie was still such a huge part of my business. I was at a point where I had to pivot again. I loved Angie but people were doing business with me, not the character. How would I manage this and have people understand that this is a real career? I work to pay my bills, and it isn't a comedy routine but rather an addition to my business.

I felt strange as if I lost myself somewhere in between Angie and Maria. I took a step back and went to my roots: learn, work, promote, build, and keep your head down to move towards the dream, the goal. The paycheck and popularity grew. It was strange to earn money because of a character I did. I felt almost guilty. I did not know why because I work my tail off recording 10 to 12 Angie videos a day, answering hundreds of daily correspondents, and traveling to meet with fans in addition to leading my team and taking care of my clients, all hands-on with no help. By choice, I did not want anyone doing my work for me, and I did not know how to delegate because I was never taught to do so. I WORKED for everything, and that silly feeling of guilt passed quickly. I was servant-driven and took care of my business team daily. I wanted success for them more than they did at the time.

I became the brand. The brand was and is ME—Maria Cyza, a human brand.

My talk, attitude, mindset, style, drive, passion, fire, personality, movements, and everything about me became THE BRAND. Organically, authentically, and genuinely relatable to everyone. Women, children, men, married, single from every culture, race, nationality, people knew who Maria Cyza was—the creator of Angie Castellano and one strong, kick-ass woman who has grit, heart, and soul. Their words, not mine, by the way.

So I know you're probably saying to yourself, "Okay, that is all great and sounds fun, but how do I brand myself? I am not a comedian; I do not have a talent like you did" Did you think I was not going to give you some tips and strategies? Come on, now, I love to share, and I want to see you rise to your greatest potential and meet those goals and dreams!

Personal branding is so much more than using strong colors, great pictures, and logos. That is marketing, not branding, which is great, but they're two different things that mesh well together.

Here we go! Reasons why you should brand yourself and not the company you represent. Keep in mind the company is amazing and has its logo, marketing, and brand all set. You are building your business, and the clients and partners you bring in are yours.

It is important for you to brand yourself because . . .

TIP 1. BRANDING SHOWS OWNERSHIP.

Showing ownership of your business builds loyalty and earns respect from clients.

TIP 2. BRANDING YOURSELF ALLOWS PEOPLE TO SEE A PERSON WHO IS RELATABLE, APPROACHABLE, AND INTERESTING.

Showing up authentically is the best way to grow in business. People can tell if someone is being fake or putting on an act. It shows up in your smile, voice, and movements. Being real, as messy as it can be sometimes, is the best way to show up.

TIP 3. BRANDING YOURSELF SETS YOU APART FROM THE REST OF THE WORLD.

Anyone can sell a product or pitch a business opportunity, but not a single person is you. You are magical, amazing, and capable of doing everything your heart desires. Show people why they should align in business with you and why they need your product.

TIP 4. YOU ARE THE BRAND! SELL YOURSELF!

People gravitate to products and opportunities that pique interest all the time. That is not a secret. So why should they buy from you or join you in business? What makes you unique? Well, in all honesty, YOU ARE UNIQUE. Unless you are an identical twin, there is no one in this world like you. That is the big secret. You and your amazing soul are original and inspirational, and the world needs people like you to show up and show them who you are. Share that each and every day authentically!

How do you brand yourself? Ok, ok that's not as hard as you may think.

Use your tools—yes, you have tools: your heart, brain, laugh, memories, life, relationships, goals, dreams, achievements, family, pets, hobbies, stories about your life, and everything that makes you who you are today! These are the connections that become real relationships. When people connect to you on this human level, it takes them back to the playground. As children, we would walk up to any kid at the park and say, "Hey, let's play tag" or "I like that ball, kick it over, let's play." We did this without reservation or fear of judgment, and guess what? We were freaking happy—ids playing, living out the day with no fear to make new friends! Your inner tools will take you back to that place as people relate to you.

Tool 1. Share your life

Tool 2. Give life and inspiration to others.

Tools 3. Serve people by showing up. Meet others' needs and solutions to problems. This creates loyalty.

Tool 4. Be Unique and allow others to see that through your eyes. When you are a little vulnerable and open, you build trustworthiness.

These key points work well when you implement your uniqueness.

- Go out and share yourself with the world.
- Be in the moment and live to inspire others.
- Connect with people to empower them.
- Be strong in your own way.
- Do not settle, get uncomfortable to grown.
- Use your inner tools to excel in your uniqueness.

I wrote this from my heart, with soul and fire in my belly.

My wish is for you to go out and become the BRAND and show this world what you are made of. I guarantee you are amazing, and we need more of that in this world!

Be Authentically Unapologetically YOU!

Be

Ready

Always

Never

Denying the power that you have inside your soul!

B.R.A.N.D

MOMENTUM MAKERS

1. **BRANDING SHOWS OWNERSHIP.** Showing ownership of your business builds loyalty and earns respect from clients.
2. **BRANDING YOURSELF ALLOWS PEOPLE TO SEE A PERSON WHO IS RELATABLE, APPROACHABLE, AND INTERESTING.** Showing up authentically is the best way to grow in business. People can tell if someone is being fake or putting on an act. It shows up in your smile, voice, and movements. Being real, as messy as it can be sometimes, is the best way to show up.
3. **BRANDING YOURSELF SETS YOU APART FROM THE REST OF THE WORLD.** Anyone can sell a product or pitch a business opportunity, but not a single person is you. You are magical, amazing, and capable of doing everything your heart desires. Show people why they should align in business with you and why they need your product.
4. **YOU ARE THE BRAND! SELL YOURSELF!** People gravitate to products and opportunities that pique interest all the time. That is not a secret. So why should they buy from you or join you in business? What makes you unique? Because YOU ARE UNIQUE. Unless you are an identical twin, there is no one in this world like you. That is the big secret. You and your amazing soul are original and inspirational, and the world needs people like you to show up and show them who you are. Share that each and every day authentically!

AMY HICKS

WHO ARE YOU?

"Today you are YOU, that is truer than true. There is no one alive who is youer than YOU."
—Dr. Seuss

So then, who are you? It seems like such a simple question, right?

WRONG.

Figuring out who we are, authentically, like who we *really* are, is hard as hell! I think it's safe to say most of us either lose sight of who we truly are or never really knew who we were in the first place. We go through of our lives conforming to the person society tells us we should be or we end up a product of our environment.

Looking back on my very first experience in network marketing, I realize it's a little ironic that an opportunity to un-conform actually resulted in me conforming more than ever. "How?" you ask.

Lemme take you back . . .

I had just jumped, both feet, into something that was not even remotely on my radar. I was intrigued by a product that made my friend's skin look flawless, and next thing I knew I was anxiously awaiting my "welcome kit." As a matter of fact, I was one of those gals who had already started selling the products before the dang thing even arrived. I guess you could say I like a good challenge and like to prove myself. But honestly, I believe it was the optimist and dreamer, in me who saw this opportunity as my way out of the corporate world and into a world of FREEDOM! Plus, like everyone, we needed more money because, you know, kids. Needless to say, I was ALL IN!

I was so all in that I did everything that everyone else in my company was doing, a true product of my environment. I sent the same scripted messages, shared the success of my "upline," wore my branded gear everywhere I went, showcased my products (even my belly) all over social media (thanks, Facebook, for the daily reminders), and "showed up to go up." If that's what made them successful, I was sure it's what would make me successful as well.

So, why wasn't I going up? I just couldn't understand why my business wasn't growing when I was doing everything everyone else was doing, which had me feeling stuck, frustrated, and discouraged. Something just didn't feel right. Eventually it dawned on me that it wasn't about growing my business—rather, it was about growing ME! That's when I started asking, "WHO THE HECK AM I?" and "WHAT IS MY PURPOSE?" And that's when I first began to seek true alignment, which I believe is one of the first milestones to building your personal brand.

Ok, let's talk about alignment. How do you know if and when you're "aligned"?

In my experience, it's not something you know but, rather, something you feel.

When I stepped outside the bubble of my team and my company, I discovered some badass women through social media who were marketing THEMSELVES and building their brands in a way that totally appealed to me! Their authenticity is what hooked me the most. They were so relatable. As a matter of fact, there were times I felt as though these women were right there next to me, sitting shotgun. It sure is incredible how much you can connect with someone you've never even met and how much you can learn through a podcast, in my case a more intentional and effective way market myself and what I have to offer. This new way was more aligned with who I am. I could feel it. I was 100% inspired and ready to put this unbeknownst mentorship into action!

It's pretty surreal, the magic that can happen when you seek true alignment and finally surrender to your "youest you." For me, it was a new opportunity that had crossed my path. It's as if God, the universe, said, "You're ready!" and presented me with something even greater than before, something that I am so genuinely passionate about. This time things would be different. It was my chance to reinvent myself, to start fresh and to implement everything I had been learning. I remember telling myself, "Amy, this is your time to SHINE!" So again, I took the risk and jumped in with both feet.

Following are two things that helped me when building the foundation of my personal brand:

#1 – YOU are your brand—people buy YOU before they invest in your product or service.

They must like you, know you, and trust you.

#2 – Defining your niche will help you effectively grow your business.

Get crystal clear on the person you help and the problem you solve.

In order for people to get to know you, you've got to let them in on your life and share your truths. You may even have to stop giving a sh*t what anyone else thinks. Those thoughts are usually our own assumptions anyway. Someone once told me, "Just take people on a journey," and that's what I've been doing ever since. A question you could ask yourself is, "Would I follow me?" What kind of value you are contributing?

Self-reflection is vital when cultivating your personal brand. Go to the place that allows you to get in tune with yourself and your thoughts. For me this is a hot soak in the tub. When I'm there, the inspiration just seems to flow effortlessly. As a bonus, I get to wash any negative energy or things that aren't serving me down the drain.

It's time you start owning who YOU are and what unique qualities, skills, and traits YOU have to offer. Stop thinking you have to do and be like everyone else. It's time to make a name for yourself, to live out your passions and personality. Demonstrate your credibility and show that you are relatable, realistic, and reliable. Be the solution for someone. Only then can you provide the necessary "tools," a.k.a. products and services. Most people don't know they need something until they know they need it, so, show up and speak up! There's always someone out there who needs to hear what you have to say. Remember this when you're contemplating hitting the "Go Live" button.

Speaking of going live, it's a MUST. People need to hear you and see you in order to trust you. They want to know you're a real person with real struggles just like they are—yep, you're gonna have to get a little vulnerable. People need to know if they feel a connection or if you're worth following.

Here's an exercise: write down the top three things that want to be known for. Think of these things as "buckets," and each bucket is a category you're passionate or knowledgeable about. For example, adventure family, holistic wellness, entrepreneur. Within each bucket you may have subcategories that you'll build upon, which becomes the content for your brand.

If you struggle with intentional content creation, use the **four Es** to help you out.

EMOTION: How or what do you want them to feel?

EDUCATION: What is it that you want them to learn from you?

ENTERTAINMENT: How will you entertain them and keep them coming back?

ENEMY: What problems/pain points are you addressing?

Pro Tip –

When creating your content, remember to write how you speak and be original. So often I see an obvious copy and paste post that sounds nothing like the person who posted it. If you see something you like from someone else, use it as inspiration but make it your own. The way you craft your message has everything to do with the tone of your personal brand and the type of person you want to attract. This is what will make you unique and set you apart.

Cool, so you're understanding the foundation of your personal brand; however, none of these things matter if you don't have an audience. I mean, you could have the most entertaining content and the most inspiring messages, but if it's not directed toward the right crowd, then it won't be nearly as powerful or could go unnoticed all together.

Hopefully this is the validity you need to narrow down or "nail your niche," as they like to say.

This is something I'm constantly striving to improve on. Since I've started being more intentional with the exact person I help and the main problem I solve, I'm not spinning my wheels nearly as much. Having a focus has allowed me to create cohesion within my brand across the various social media platforms. I've also noticed much more authentic engagement and a higher conversion rate, in turn growing my business.

Luckily for all of us, there is an abundance of social media platforms—free exposure, you guys! Don't ever take that for granted, because it may not be free forever. I'm a firm believer that you must master at least one platform. Dabbling in them all, here and there, isn't going to create a strong presence, and you'll just get lost in the social sea. Be willing to take the time to grow and nurture a quality network of people, your community, your tribe, who want exactly what you have to offer. This foundational step to building your personal brand cannot be skipped. Go where your niche audience is most likely to be hanging out.

The following questions will help you to narrow down your ideal client:

- What is the age range and gender of this person?
- What are some personality traits of this person?
- What are this person's interests?
- What are this person's struggles?
- What hashtags might this person be using?

Now let's talk about progress over perfection.

Have you ever stalled out because you were so hung up on the perfect topic for your live video and looking perfectly put together, the perfect name for your group, or the perfect font. I'm sure you can think of more. I'm going to take some pressure off you, ok? There are people who are way less qualified than you are, and they're already doing it. So JUST START!

Your brand can (and likely will) change and evolve, so it doesn't have to be perfect. Be willing to learn as you go, or grow. Be willing to start messy. One of the things that has led me to where I am today is having the courage to start before I'm ready. It's taken five years of putting myself out there and trying things to realize what works and what doesn't, what brings me joy and what doesn't, what people want to see and what they don't. Part of the growth process is failing forward and learning. The longer you do it, the better you'll be—strive to become a PRO! And when that embarrassing Facebook memory from the past pops up, you'll be humbled and proud to see how far you've come. You'll be glad that you continued to show up and push through despite the one like and five views, because when you're on a growth journey, there is no finish line. We are always evolving and improving. Just remember to never lose sight of who you truly are, what lights you up, and what brings you JOY! P.S. If you aren't having FUN doing it, you aren't doing it right.

I hope by now you're overflowing with inspiration, your brain is churning out the ideas, and you're ready to express yo-self! While everything outlined above will help you establish the foundation of your personal brand, I'd like to leave you with a few more *pro tips* and some creative tangibles. Sometimes it's the little touches that can make a big difference.

Yes, we're living in a digital world, but never underestimate the value of a physical business card. Allow this card to represent the style, tone, and intention of your brand. Your personal photo, colors, and logo can speak volumes. And remember, your logo can simply be a stylized version of your name. Leave a lasting impression, stay top of mind, and let your potential clients know where they can easily find you.

Selfie tutorials and iPhones have come a long way, but if you want to be a "professional," then I suggest you invest in a few professional headshots. This doesn't have to cost an arm and a leg, but they should be high quality, involve great lighting and allow for your personality and confidence to shine through. The way you present and position yourself is a direct reflection of your brand. Put your best face forward—you're worth it!

While a personal website can be effective, it's not necessary. Most of us already have a personal link to our company site, so you could easily purchase your own branded URL link and have it forward to your company site. If you have website links (products/services) that fall under your personal brand umbrella, check out LinkTree to house them all in one easy-to-find location. Simple navigation and clear, concise information can often be more important than the pretty colors and graphics.

Creating "own-able content" is key to establishing recognition. A quick and easy hack that everyone can do is to find a quote that is aligned with your Personal Brand and recreate it in your own style rather than sharing it or posting a screen shot. Your goal is to empower others to share YOUR content. Apps like WordSwag and Canva make it simple to create unique, custom content. Use consistent colors and fonts, change up the wording slightly, and be sure to brand your image. I like to discretely include my personal handle, brand name, or a repeating hashtag for additional brand recognition.

*Remember, people buy people. Make your mission known and become an expert at telling your story—over and over. It's YOUR STORY, and no one can tell it quite like you can. The more you do it, the more comfortable and fluid it will become and the more known you will become. You may even want to work with a public speaking coach; doing so has helped me tremendously. Be sure to have a few versions of your story, both short and long. Write it, speak it, TikTok it. Think about where you were, where you are now, and where you're headed. It's time to bring some people along your journey and INSPIRE the f*ck out of them. YOU are the cornerstone of your Personal Brand, and you have so much to offer.* ***Be confident, be bold, BE YOU, and OWN IT!***

If any of this resonates with you, and I sure hope it does, then I strongly encourage you to start putting it into practice TODAY! Start before you're ready. I promise that if you do, "You'll be on your way up! You'll be seeing great sights! You'll join the high fliers who soar to high heights."

I can't wait to watch YOU soar!

MOMENTUM MAKERS

1. **YOU ARE YOUR BRAND – PEOPLE BUY YOU BEFORE THEY INVEST IN YOUR PRODUCT OR SERVICE.** Start owning who YOU are and what unique qualities, skills and traits YOU have to offer. In order for people to get to know you, you've got to let them in on your life and share your truths. They must like you, know you, and trust you.

2. **DEFINING YOUR NICHE WILL HELP YOU EFFECTIVELY GROW YOUR BUSINESS.** Get crystal clear on the person you help and the problem you solve. Being more intentional with the exact person you help and the main problem you solve will keep you from spinning your wheels as much. Having a focus will allow you to create cohesion within your brand across the various social media platforms.

3. **YOUR BRAND CAN (AND LIKELY WILL) CHANGE AND EVOLVE, SO IT DOESN'T HAVE TO BE PERFECT.** Be willing to learn as you go, or grow. Be willing to start messy. One of the things that has led me to where I am today is having the courage to start before I'm ready. So JUST START.

4. **IF YOU WANT TO BE A "PROFESSIONAL," THEN INVEST IN A FEW PROFESSIONAL HEADSHOTS.** They should be high-quality, involve great lighting, and allow for your personality and confidence to shine through. The way you present and position yourself is a direct reflection of your brand.

MOMENTUM MAKERS

5. **WHEN IT COMES TO CREATING CONTENT, REMEMBER THE 4 E:**

   Emotion: How or what do you want them to feel?

   Education: What is it that you want them to learn from you?

   Entertainment: How will you entertain them and keep them coming back?

   Enemy: What problems/pain points are you addressing?

GERALDINE DE PABLO

YOU ARE YOUR OWN BRAND

We all want to be rich, thin, popular, and handsome, but why is it that not too many people get what they want? The truth is that more than 50% of the world's population live in miserable conditions, 45% live day-to-day, and only 5% get all the money. Why is this true if we live in such an abundant world, and what if there is an industry that can improve your life?

I'm Geraldine de Pablo, and I'm happily married to my best friend, Paul Rammeloo. We have worked in network marketing for a little more than 15 years and truly believe that to become successful in this profession you have to create your personal brand—you have to build a mentality of abundance at the same time that you work to have a solid organization.

When we started this amazing adventure, we both had good jobs. I worked as a psychologist, and Paul was an engineer, but even when we had the money, we didn't have the time we wanted, which is so important to everything in our life. So we started looking for time and financial freedom, and that is when I decided to start my career in MLM.

Network marketing was really hard in the beginning, and we had a learning curve, but we realized that we had to be trainable, coachable, and willing to change our thoughts and beliefs in ourselves. We had a lot to learn but we were very resilient, and we have found that even though we've been doing this line of work for years, we are still learning. We have learned that we needed to be coachable and learn from the people that have done it.

The most important thing that you need to consider about being a networker (especially for couples who are building a business together) is to build your thought-life, to believe that you are worth it. You can have everything that you want if you feel you deserve it.

When you start building, do everything you can to support each other and to believe in yourself because you will create your reality. We always encourage people to "Never stop working on yourself" because it is so worth it to pay the price of investing in yourself when you see the results.

We all have the right to succeed in life. We all have the right to live in love and abundance. We all have the same opportunity to create a presence for ourselves, a personal brand that is unique to each one of us. It is our natural birthright. If you don´t believe that you deserve it, you have to transform your thinking. When we focused our trainings with our team on this, the magic started happening.

I realized that network marketing was the best vehicle to break these paradigms—that the true power is within ourselves. I believe that if we want to receive, we have to give; we have to help others to believe in themselves and develop the potential that we all have within each one of us. What I LOVE about my business is that for me to win, someone else has to win—something that only this industry can give us.

This is an incredible industry, and everyone can make it, but you have to believe it and you have to work it. Thanks to this industry, we have been able to change and transform how we live, not only in a financial way but in the transformation we had when we discovered the potential that we have in who we are.

I have been empowering individuals to become the creator of their own lives and how to learn to love themselves and their circumstances regardless of their experiences in life. I have shared with them that they are unique with a purpose and have helped them to share their uniqueness with others; therefore, in many cases, creating a brand for themselves.

I have taught many people the ability to enable themselves to access the unlimited sources of inspiration, strength, and clarity that lie within them, along with building the capacity to understand, forgive, accept, and have an appreciation for every part of themselves and their lives—to embrace peace as a natural state and recognize that life does not occur outside of us but rather inside of us.

Our lives and the way we want to live them are in our hands. The majority of people are victims of their own thoughts; you need to be able to explore where those thoughts were created and enhance your ability to rebuild your own self-concept and embrace abundance, embracing who you are as a person, parent, partner, entrepreneur, etc.

We all have the capacity to transforming every painful, scary, and stressful experience into a meaningful, courageous, and inspiring life from which others can be inspired and encouraged.

Our happiness is our own responsibility; our success in MLM is our own responsibility. If we want to be a new leader or reach a new rank in our company, we need to become our best versions of ourselves and vibrate with these goals to obtain them while remaining coherent with the universe and ourselves.

But you must keep in mind that this is not an easy profession. If someone tells you that you will start making money just by calling your contacts, they're lying to you. It will take some time, especially if you are new to this industry, for you to start earning money. It is not easy, but it is possible.

Network marketing is not a business for everyone. But we can have success when we challenge ourselves and face the fact that our success depends on us; we challenge ourselves while "sailing" in a sea of "no's" from which we must learn.

Be prepared for the rejections, but don't give up. Take the "negatives" as learning and be resilient. Don't take it personally, and above all, accept and recognize that not everyone is a prospect. Consider that not everyone is at the moment adapting, nor are they willing to face the challenge themselves. They all want to be successful but do not want to pay the price for success.

You must change your mindset. Learn to trust, believe, and work as a team, and accept guidance, taking advantage of all the support that the people you work with can offer you. Believe that you really deserve to have that financial freedom; be emotionally and mentally prepared, by investing in your personal growth on a daily basis.

When you start to get the "yes's" and your downline begins to grow, this is the moment when you must begin to create a support system, training, and meetings for your team. This will help the duplication to happen more quickly.

I always say not to work too hard to convince anyone to join you because if you convince someone to do the business, you will have to carry them forever. They will hold you responsible if they fail and blame you, and if they succeed, they will not remember you.

With all I am saying, I am trying to open a new window of insight for you as to how capable you are of living a life in which you do not NEED anyone else to be successful but ourselves and a new vision of creating success along with abundance by deciding to do it.

Along with empowering a new version of us that allows us to be independent and successful individuals, we must also become our own brand, compelling others to follow not necessarily the company we represent but who we are. A very effective way to do this and recognize the real thoughts and ideas about ourselves is by taking a look at our reality.

You get in life what you believe you should get. This doesn't always happen consciously—most of the time, it happens in a very deep-down subconscious way. That is why most people in the network marketing industry emphasize what they are selling instead of who they are and why others should follow after them. They don't believe they deserve a personal brand, which can be a disaster if/when they ever leave their company for another. If you really want to be successful in your business, you should work on it as it's the only option you have. Trust and believe that it is possible to succeed if you want it to.

We learned that the most important thing is that you must give everything you can to your team. Give your time, your support, your knowledge, your energy and everything that helps others to grow, but the most important thing is to do it while still being yourself. Do it with an attitude of service and everything will change; you will create synergy in your team and everything will begin to flow.

You must have a mind and heart of success; the higher your rank, the more commitment and service you will have to give. Rank does not define you, your actions do. How much do you help your team and celebrate their achievements?

We need to understand our weaknesses and strengths as well as those of others, a key point to achieving strength in your team. Recognize that you are in a process of learning to embrace your life as it has been. Recognize your strengths but also your weaknesses, and it is important to recognize the stratospheric difference.

People who love themselves recognize where they are. They have a solid respect for themself, acknowledge that they have much strength, and are proud of themself while also remaining aware of their many weaknesses. They work every day at being the best version of themselves. People with high self-esteem love serving others because they understand the benefits that the industry offers them, and understand that to grow personally, they need to help other members of the team develop and grow. They are someone who has the vision and the skills to become a leader.

You have to believe that your company will provide and support you at the same time that your team will do the same for you in every situation. You can also have an amazing support group that will help and support you in every step. You need to believe in yourself and in your company, which is the key to creating your own family and brand in this industry. I really believe this. For me, it is the most important reason to introduce myself as a proud network marketer and is so crucial to creating your personal brand.

When creating your personal brand, you need to consider that there is so much involved not only in the company but in yourself—there is social media, the technical part, the products, the lifestyle, and all the other things that you need to build it.

It is important to know the products as well as the benefits and the history of the company you are in. You should be enthusiastic, a good salesperson, a closer, and a recruiter, but beyond that, it is more important that you build a brand, a name, and a reputation. These aspects do not define the quality of the company you represent or the products they offer, but they will define who you are regardless of which company you are in.

When you understand the importance of this point is when you have understood that you are the best product you have to offer your prospects. This will give you the opportunity to know that the people on your team are in it for you, for who you are, and for what you represent.

You must help people see in you the product, a unique product that no other person can give them. That is the reason why you should create your own brand, because when prospecting, in addition to talking about the benefits of your product, the advantages of your company, and the compensation plan, you add the value of your own person as a leader. Remember that people do not join a company because of its products or its compensation plan but because of the trust and security of the members of their organization. You can change companies, but your leadership remains intact, and you can take your team to another company that suits your needs. Build that leadership that you have within you, which is so necessary for this type of business.

Your personal brand is your story, your name, who you are, what you represent, what you know how to do, your values, your way of thinking and doing things—your reputation.

Business has changed and is now increasingly personal. People want to do business with real people. Your prospects pay attention to your face, your personality, your beliefs, and the energy you transmit by sharing the business opportunity. They do not pay attention to a product, a logo, or your company offices; they need to know you to know if they identify with you or not. They must trust you to be able to buy from you or enter your business.

By serving others in the way you were uniquely meant to, you automatically create your own "brand." No one else can do it quite like you can. Those who know you will know who it is you really are and develop a sense of whether or not they want to board your train for success. This is crucial in identifying someone who is really at peace with their own life.

We have to remember that no one can give what they do not have, so if a person does not have genuine love and respect for themselves, they will never be able to truly love any other individual. A person who is in love with themselves will radiate that love and will live in service to others. Likewise, you need to build your personal brand on the internet, but you must be very careful when you do it because what you show in your virtual life must be congruent with your real life. Today, more than ever, people want to connect with people; we have the need to create an emotional bond because in this way we feel that there is transparency in what you are offering.

Once you have created your brand, it will be much easier to do your business, because now you represent yourself. You will create trust and the recognition you need to be able to affiliate people to use your product, your service, or your company.

Your personal brand is very easy to share since all you do is share who you are, what your interests are, your way of thinking, what you do, and how you do it. This is what people are looking for, to connect with them and their interests.

Creating our personal brand allowed us to become "Diamonds" twice in our company, achieving an unprecedented achievement. People decide to be part of our team because they wanted to be a part of who we are, not for the company or the products, which makes us really grateful.

Congruence in this industry is very important because you will receive exactly what you give; if we don't have congruence with what we do, we won't be able to achieve the results we expect. People aren't going to do what you tell them to do but what they see you do. If you want your team committed, you must be committed to your business first.

You can´t receive unless you give, which is so important to building your brand. You need to invest in yourself; financial success will come much faster when you give value to yourself and your personal brand.

MOMENTUM MAKERS

1. **WE ALL HAVE THE RIGHT TO SUCCEED IN LIFE.** We all have the same opportunity to create a presence for ourselves, a personal brand that is unique to each one of us. If you don´t believe that you deserve it, you have to transform your thinking.

2. **YOU NEED TO BE TRAINABLE, COACHABLE, AND WILLING TO CHANGE YOUR THOUGHTS AND BELIEVE IN YOURSELF.** Be resilient and learn from the people that have done it before you.

3. **TO CREATE YOUR PERSONAL BRAND, YOU HAVE TO BUILD A MENTALITY OF ABUNDANCE AT THE SAME TIME THAT YOU WORK TO HAVE A SOLID ORGANIZATION.** Give your team your time, your support, your knowledge, your energy, and everything that helps others to grow, and do it while still being yourself.

4. **NEVER STOP WORKING ON YOURSELF.** Believe that you are worth it and that you can have everything you want because you deserve it.

5. **CONGRUENCE BETWEEN YOUR PERSONAL BRAND AND WHO YOU REALLY ARE IS VERY IMPORTANT IN THIS INDUSTRY.** Your personal brand is your story, your name, who you are, what you represent, what you know how to do, your values, your way of thinking and doing things—your reputation.

CAMILLE HAMMERICH

USE YOURSELF

You are unique. You have a great story. And you are on a mission on this planet.

When I found my mission in this world, everything became so much easier, including my network marketing business.

My mission is to help as many people as possible to live their dreams, and when I became a single mom, my mission was to show my son that he should live his life just the way he wanted to.

You can't fake passion.

I was brought up by two people who always followed their passions in life. They always told me that I should follow my dream and always should believe in myself. When I was 10 years old, my parents got divorced, and they choose to separate me and my brother. This was heartbreaking both for me and my mom, with whom I lived. It made me very insecure, and my self-esteem hit rock bottom. I missed my dad and brother every day. It was a very difficult time in my life, and it made me even more introverted than I already was. I was the tallest girl in class and got bullied. Puberty was a very difficult time for me.

As I got older, I did a giant soul searching, and my self-esteem grew. I found the belief and realized that if just one other person had done it, so could I. When I made the decision of living my dream and believed that I could, things really started to happen for me.

Network marketing is so much more than making a lot of money.

Marry your process and remember to divorce the results.

My passion is to help as many people as possible to grow and become their best version of themselves. When they become their best version, they will believe that they can help others, too.

It all starts with belief. When you believe in yourself, you will take action, and with the action comes excitement and then momentum.

Who are you, and how do you want the world to see you?

Two questions that you need to take a hard and thorough look at.

Personal branding is ALL about you; therefore, you need to figure out almost everything about yourself. I'm now in my late 40s, and I know almost everything there is to know about myself: my dreams, what drives me, what are my strengths and weaknesses are, and how I enrich people`s lives.

The most important tool you have is yourself and your story, and we all have a story. In network marketing, you have a story about why you joined the business and a story about the product. Tell your story and use your story to build your business—this is the strongest tool you have.

Branding yourself often makes you a good storyteller. You are telling about your life, network marketing, dreams, vision, your story, and so much more.

When I found out that ENVY could be a positive thing, it really turned things around in my world. Look at this perspective. Hopefully, you are in the right state of mind and can be happy for the person who obtains the things you want. Being envious only confirms that YOU want to obtain that position and achievement. Use this strong feeling as your driving force.

Another major feeling is PATIENCE, although many find patience to be a strong opponent and struggle to have it. We all want success to happen now and no later than yesterday! But things take time. In order to have patience, you need to learn how to get on top of it and stay focused. Imagine if a big tree did not have strong roots underneath when a storm came—the tree would fall. A strong tree needs strong roots, and that takes time. Growing patience works the same way—it takes time but gives you stability when the storms of life come.

Have you made your DECISION? Can you feel your decision and your WHY? Because then you are ready to take action on your personal branding on social media.

I have been in this industry for over 30 years but have only made a really good living from it in the last 7 years. It was when I realized that I should promote myself that network marketing became a lifestyle and more than a job.

I have achieved Double Diamond with my last two companies and have earned more money than I have ever could have before. The first time I hit the Double Diamond rank was "the old fashion way" (the way some are still doing it): copy a text and asking a lot of people if they want to join the business. It took me 5 months to become Double Diamond, but half a year later almost all of my downline were inactive. One of the explanations was that they joined the business because of my energy and not because they really wanted to do the business.

The second time I hit the Double Diamond rank it took me a bit longer—almost a full year—but mainly because I was doing attraction marketing and not pushing people. To this day I have not lost the rank, only some of my downline have left, and business is still growing. This time people joined the company with their own energy.

My favorite social media platform is Facebook. My profile on Facebook is my business card—where people go to learn about me. I am very active on a daily basis. I do one to four posts daily on my private profile and one or two in my groups/on my business page. I have a DMO, Daily Method of Operating, and I do it every day . . . every week . . . every month . . . and every year . . . persistence.

I build relationships from my heart and only work with people I want to have in my life. I try to give a lot of value through advice to everybody on social media. Network marketing is about building relationships and talking to people.

For many years I have had the pleasure of giving a lot of motivational talks around my country, Denmark. I have met a lot of people who later on became distributors and friends. I speak about going for the goals in your life and finding the courage to go for the dream. This is, of course, a great way to make new relationships, and I am persistent to reach out for their friendship after I speak.

I am also an author. I wrote my first book in 2018, *Get Yourself a Job*. The title is a sentence I often hear as an entrepreneur. People would say to me, "You are a single mom, should you not get a real job instead . . ." My son actually gave me the title of the book. At that time we didn´t have that much money to travel. He was about seven years old, and he'd been in school for a couple of years at that point when he said to me, "Mom, why don't you just get a real job so we can have more money for living?" It was then that I realized what he was being told in school: sit down, learn about a lot, get an education, get a job, save for a pension, and when you receive a pension you will have all the time to travel and have fun. I told him that I did have a job and that I wanted to spend time with him instead of having a bigger house or more traveling around the world.

The book was about my first 46 years and about who I am as a person—it was to let people know more about me and perhaps find me able to help them with their dream and how I continue to have the courage to keep on living the life that I want. Writing a book is a very positive way of branding yourself.

My second book was also released in 2018 and was about network marketing and how to build a team by using attraction marketing. Both books are pieces in my personal branding. My network marketing book, *Allow Yourself to Dream Big – That Is Network Marketing and How Do You Get Success* is now translated into English, German, and Spanish.

I recommend for everybody to write a book on anything that inspires them or to write their own stories. Through your book, you can connect to people who share your interest and, at the same time, brand yourself. Everybody should write his or her own story and save it for their kids or print it and use it for branding. I would have loved to have had my mom's story written down. She died in 2013.

Through the process of being an entrepreneur, I have really gotten to know myself. I knew that I had to work on my belief and my self-esteem. You have to work on yourself and become the person you want to be before you can ask anyone else to do the same. It`s like with kids—people do what you are doing not what you are telling them to do. Monkey see, monkey do.

Once I realized that I could do this business by branding myself, it was so much easier to post on social media. My WHY and the vision for my life became clear.

I want to lift the industry. I want more people to have the same success that I am having.

It is very important that you remain yourself. Don't think you should be anybody other than you! You are unique, and if you don't think so yet, you should start working on that mindset. Your self-esteem should be in order. You have to believe that you are worth following in life and business, otherwise, people will sense that you don't have that confidence, and I believe that you will struggle to build your organization.

It takes money to make money. You probably already know this quote. But once I realized that I needed to spend money on myself by using a coach, taking courses on personal development, and buying books about the subject, that was when I got my self-esteem in order. We often use money on education but not on self-education.

I believe in the law of attraction. I really believe that you can attract anything you want. But before the law of attraction comes the law of frequencies. If you don't believe in yourself, you are sending out the wrong frequencies and the law of attraction won't really work.

You are one-of-a-kind, and when you realize it, the world of Network Marketing will open up.

DMO:

I congratulate everybody on their birthday with a 1-minute video, where I sing a birthday song. And at the same time, I post a birthday card on their private Facebook page.

I do Live from my private page two to six times a week.

I share my life and private life with everyone on my page by posting portraits that amplify me as a real and authentic person. What you see is what you get.

MOMENTUM MAKERS

1. **ALWAYS BE YOURSELF.** Stay true to others and yourself. When you believe in yourself, you will take action, and with the action comes excitement and then momentum.

2. **LOVE WHAT YOU DO AND BE PASSIONATE ABOUT YOUR PRODUCT AND TEAM.** The most important tool you have is yourself and your story, and we all have a story. In network marketing, you have a story about why you joined the business and a story about the product. Tell your story and use your story to build your business—this is the strongest tool you have.

3. **WRITE A BOOK ON ANYTHING THAT INSPIRES YOU OR WRITE YOUR OWN STORIES.** Through your book, you can connect to people who share your interest and, at the same time, brand yourself.

4. **HAVE A DMO (DAILY METHOD OF OPERATING).** Do it every day . . . every week . . . every month . . . and every year . . . persistence.

5. **ALWAYS REACH OUT FOR HELP.** Spend money on yourself by using a coach, taking courses on personal development, and buying books about the subject. . . . not just when you have doubts in yourself or in your business, but all the time. Be an unbeatable TEAM.

EMILY ROBERTS

MASTERING THE ART OF STORY TELLING

When I think of personal branding, I think of actual branding. I'm from the South, and in Texas farmers often brand their cattle, and when you brand an animal, you leave a mark of significance—to those the farmers, it's a mark of ownership. Hey y'all, I'm Emily, a professional storyteller, and mother of three who has found simple and smart ways to be yourself while also working towards being successful in your business. If the farmer analogy gave you any indication of my personality or whereabouts, think again. My brain can be so random; I have just learned how to own it and be proud of what it's done in leadership, life, business, and even my own personal branding. Analogies have been a part of my story-telling for the last six years, and I believe have helped my audience understand me better than ever! I can't wait to show you how to be more of you so you can focus on your current strengths to build a brand you and your network love.

But for starters, here's the thing, friends: this ain't your grandpa's farm—this is your business. This is the legacy that you will leave behind for your babies and their grandbabies. This is how you "leave your mark" on the world. This is your platform and how you confidently help them solve their problems while you wash dishes, change diapers, and change your life. Your brand is what represents you, explains your stances, tells stories, and is basically a logo for your life. For example, you could see the Coca-Cola logo and pinpoint what it represents without ever seeing their name, right? That's the brand they've built—the color scheme, the logo, the catchy commercial songs, heck even the Christmas Polar bear most of us know and recognize. That's what we're going to dissect here. Your logo is your face—show more of it. Your slogan is your "why" and what you're working towards. Your marketing materials and commercials are your social media posts and platforms that reach more people and show off your creativity. Chances are you already have a brand and didn't even realize it.

In this chapter, you will learn four ways to personally brand yourself, your business, and the stories you're trying to sell. Yes, sell. That is not a typo, friend. You're selling the solutions to the problems others have. It doesn't even matter the product you sell, the solution you share, or the supplement you use; the consumer has to get it from somewhere. That somewhere should be you. So what makes them pick you out of the entire worldwide search engine of social sharers on and offline? Your brand.

I've been in this industry for six and a half years, and in that time I've experienced three long-distance military deployments, two pregnancies, two cross-country moves, family loss, prenatal loss, as well as financial hardships, and even a worldwide pandemic. Even though times were tough, I realized that I was still me and still had solutions for people's problems with the product that I offered them. I still had value, humor, wit, knowledge, and excitement to discuss with my growing audience. Neither then nor now was the time to stop, give up, or simmer on the idea of "stepping on toes"; no I finish what I start and wanted to confidently help others do the same.

For example, I mentioned our cross-country move; military friends, this was PCS season, and I was two months into my network marketing business. I had built this extraordinary team in California only to hear we would be leaving in two weeks for Virginia. I had never been to the east coast. This could have derailed me and my business, but I instead looked forward to planting new seeds and creating new relationships somewhere new. So how do you stay true to your brand when life is chaotic? You schedule it and talk about the "busyness."

I documented what that was like with a young baby; I shared how I could work my business from hotels, parking lots, gas stations, and even from the back seat when our baby was hungry. I told stories about the late-night drives, asked questions to engage my audience about where we were headed and what to expect. I even talked about how as a military spouse moving was second nature and offered value by sharing our top moving and packing tips. I used this time to get vulnerable and connect with those who were following me online until I could plant new roots in a new community. My company is wellness-based, so I would talk about healthier alternatives on the road and show pictures of our meals and how my products fit into our chaotic schedule, and I encouraged my audience that they could stay on track even amidst a busy season of life. Since I was so open about what I was going through or experiencing, I have made new relationships with others who may experience this later in life, but because I've consistently showed up, they knew who to turn to and trust when it came to certain topics. That just solidifies the brands I've built. My brands aligned with motherhood, military, my faith, and my postpartum journey.

Let's dive into what this would look like for you and the brand you're developing. Now would be a good time to grab that pen and highlighter because this is my first suggestion, folks.

First off, know who you are. Even if you're growing into your best self, discovering raw truths, digging up past regrets, know that. Own that. Memorize the energy those memories and situations made you feel, then share those experiences. That *is* you. Those moments have shaped you, slapped you, and sewn you together to make you, YOU. I bought my son a Dr. Suess book, *Happy Birthday to You*, that delivers an all-time favorite quote: "No one is Youer than You."

So often we copy and paste on social media because we borrow ideas and thoughts, but have you ever realized you're doing that in real life, too? You start acting like your coworkers. Stay-at-home parents, you may even be eating and acting like your kiddos—possibly whiny, argumentative, or flat-out exhausted. This can affect your brand if you allow it, or you can grow that vulnerability muscle and share how you're embracing it. Your brand IS you. It's the five people you spend your time with. It's what you wear. It's how you react. It's how you connect. It's how you listen and speak. So be yourself and own it. Know that no one is you, and let that ignite the ambition inside of you.

Secondly, your brand tells a story. For example, I mentioned loving analogies. When I hear a story, an analogy will pop into my head so I can retell the story and make it more relatable. It's now become a part of my brand because when I tell stories, so many listening have "a-ha" moments when I share through that analogy lens. One of my favorite Facebook "lives" came from being on the road at a hotel in downtown San Antonio on the Riverwalk. The hotel room we stayed in backed up to a construction site. My boys were 2 years old and 9 months old and loved trucks of all sizes. We would watch the tractors, bulldozers, cement trucks, and excavators work for hours. Watching these trucks inspired me to tell my own story of success, which was hard for me to talk about at that time. I used a real-life story about how I have always felt "under construction" or like a "work in progress." I shared some personal mindset struggles and how God was the greatest excavator of all time, cleaning up the messes I had made in my life so graciously. I continued on and explained why we were even on that balcony to begin with. We were in Texas because my opportunity and business allowed my husband the freedom to leave the Marine Corps ten years earlier than we had ever planned and he was excited to explore opportunities in Texas. It was a full-circle moment for me as I sat with my babies in my lap on top of that cold, metal patio chair. I could truly inspire more moms to step up and out in faith for their kids or hardworking spouses and not feel held back because of them. You see, these stories weren't just a part of my brand; they were also a way for me to process emotion, cope, and communicate with those watching to see what was to come next in my business and life.

As you're reading this some of you may be thinking, "Oh, heck no—I hate talking about myself." Or "Do I really have to open up more?" Maybe the thought of that is making you physically ill, so let me encourage you. When was the last time you looked in the mirror? Did you like your reflection? Did you smile? Grimace? Dance? Maybe you let out a long sigh as you glanced over at the scale in the corner?

Friends, you were fearfully and wonderfully made with a divine purpose and intricate story to share to a world full of darkness. Your hope, your desire to be better, is what shines so brightly and ignites a fire of change. I mean, somebody crank up Rachel Platten's "Fight Song," because I am fired up right now. You're reading this book because you felt a nudge, a shift that perhaps greatness was calling your name and that you were made for more. Knowing that, take this advice I received from a business mentor within my company; she often reminded me to be "a connector-of-the-heart, not just a teller-of-the-things." Anyone can word-vomit fun facts, dimensions, adjectives, and prices, but that's not what always seals the deal. No, what connects them to you is the story—it's the reason why some songs we can't stand until we watch the music video. Or when we assume a movie will be an epic fail based on the title alone. What would a movie of your life look like? What character are you? How can you explain these life events or tragedies to become a connector-of-the-heart?

Personal stories tell us details that aren't on the price tag. Read that again. I would often hear in coaching sessions from clients and team members, "So I just went grocery shopping; that's all I did today—I'm supposed to tell a story about that?" YES! See anyone? Did your child act a fool? Was your favorite soup on sale? There is always a way to offer value in what you share.

Y'all, personal branding IS storytelling. It's the same story with the same characters being retold every single day with new and different adjectives. See, point number one about knowing yourself and where you come from or this second point is going to be really hard on some of y'all. I know, I get it. You're sitting there with that highlighter clenched between your teeth or on the desk next to you. You're so close to that promotion. Your wife is about to have that baby. Your father-in-law recently passed away. This is your fifth company in seven years. You feel disconnected, misplaced, and unwanted. You feel rejected and like no one listens. You're burying yourself into this book to deflect from the story you should be out living so that you can start sharing with the audience you're supposed to be connecting with.

Basically, I'm suggesting that you start documenting and stop obsessing over creating a "perfect brand." You aren't perfect, so why expect your brand to be? Most of us have shifted to an E-commerce-style of business to attract and reach more people; however, we have subconsciously developed this irrational fear that we are constantly competing with those around us, so having new, outstanding content is a must. What if I told you that was a limiting belief? One of my favorite branding mentors and dear friends of mine is Rebekah Fowlkes. She actually offers simple solutions to branding online every day and taught me this skill. She said, "Stop worrying about creating the perfect post with the perfect picture and perfect caption and just document what's happening in your world and post about that! People will find value in feeling like they know you and what you stand for." I just LOVE that. Zig Ziglar says, "If people like you, they will listen to you, but if they trust you, they'll do business with you." Isn't this what branding is all about? They chose you because they saw vulnerable, consistent you, showing up and being yourself.

Now that leads me to point three, *trying on perspectives*. You are made up of many seasons of life, right? You have years of experiences you've witnessed or been through, and with that comes a trigger to how you respond, how you tell your story, and how you keep sharing stories.

For instance, find something above you want to apply in that next meeting, social media post, or your next YouTube video? Do it. Apply it. Try it on like you're in a dressing room.

Go with me here: there is nothing more agonizing than trying on clothes during the winter months. Statistically, we are fatter, more stressed out, and in the south, it's 40° when you wake up and 85° by lunchtime, so if you're like me, you're probably sweaty, too. However, we still shop. We still try on our top picks from those shiny, over-packed, silver racks. We brush elbows with strangers in department after department looking for clothes that make us feel good, look good, and boost our confidence levels.

So that's what I'm saying. I want you to TRY ON new perspectives every day. Tell a story from a *different point of you.* Like your 8-year-old self. Like you, pre-divorce. Like you, 57 lbs. lighter. How does that feel? What's changed? What's stayed consistent? When we try on new perspectives, we invite in new audiences, and that's how our personal brand expands as well as our network. Apply new perspectives to your brand like you apply sunscreen. ALL OVER AND IN EVERY CREVICE of your life and business. Not just on social media. Not just at the dinner table. Not just in your bathroom in front of the mirror. Try it on and apply it so that you uncover what's really on your mind, what sets you back, what has limited your beliefs, and secretly stays a hot topic in your brain. Lastly, since you have now learned that you are your brand, your life stories make up that brand and your different stages of life offer a flood of perspective to your now growing network.

"So now what, Emily?" you're probably thinking. "I'm not so sure about this," you may be doubting. Now you put action behind these tips, you dog-ear this chapter and you do what you do best. My fourth branding suggestion is this, *know your strengths.* BE YOURSELF. What are you GREAT at? Notice how I didn't say what you're good at. I'm good at blowing a bubble with my gum, but I am great at using analogies to reference significance in my stories. Gary Vaynerchuk says, "Maybe don't call it social media. Just be a human and tell your story." *I agree, Gary—that's what I'm trying to teach these guys.* If you want to perfect your brand, you're not listening. If you want to make cute graphics and have a pretty Instagram feed, you don't get it. That's not what your brand is about. If you want to influence people, be consistent and help them first. Find a way, every single day, to retell your story, your breaking point, your near-death experience, your sick and tired of being sick and tired moment. Just share it. Even if one person likes it, reads it, listens or shares it, that's one more person who has heard it. Knowing your strengths is a great way to show off how your solution solves many problems. Your solution is your business, by the way; your brand just explains the different varieties of problems that led you to this solution.

Remember that cattle farmer from earlier? I'm sure the first time he branded a cow he felt guilty, but I also think he stood a little bit taller. With consistency comes confidence, and that's what people buy into. They buy into the most confident version of you that you put out there. So I leave you with this question, what story will you share first?

As you mentally take notes and prepare for the chapter that follows, I hope you realize you do, in fact, offer so much value to the world and that your growing business will make a difference. It "feels" small, and sometimes as you're discovering your brand you may even feel like "a lot," but it's so worth it to look back and see what you've created. Your brand is found in the details, the small bloopers of your life's seasons. Your brand may bring in sales or close deals, but most of all I hope it provides specific details for the world to get to know you first.

"Personal stories tell us details that aren't on the price tag."
—Emily Roberts

MOMENTUM MAKERS

1. **KNOW WHO YOU ARE, YOUR LIKES AND DISLIKES; HAVE A STANCE AND STICK WITH IT.** Confidence creates consumers. When you know who you are, what you want, and who you are talking to, you solidify an audience that will continue to grow because of referrals. When you fake it, you lack integrity and your brand falls apart, just like mixing puzzle pieces together from five different puzzle boxes. It won't work. This step is so important, so who are you and what problem are you solving?

2. **TELL YOUR STORY AND KEEP TELLING IT.** Pretend that when someone finds you, your website, or your social media that it's a first date. Open up, offer some vulnerability, and stay tactful and truthful. Your brand will always tell your story, so what chapter are you on? What chapter just ended?

3. **IT'S IMPORTANT TO VISIT THE PAST ONLY TO *TRY ON* THAT VERSION OF YOU AND THE PERSPECTIVE WITH IT.** It's important not to be some arrogant expert but to relive your real-life examples for those currently going through that struggle. For example, by trying on an old problem with your teenage mentality, you can walk a current teenager through what feels like to them, a crisis, and help them find resolution in their sucky season. What perspective can you share from in your next venture?

MOMENTUM MAKERS

4. **KNOW YOUR STRENGTHS AND BE YOURSELF.** Consistency builds trust. As you influence others with this constant behavior and networking, you will learn your audience's needs and wants. You can offer solutions to every problem with your own advice confidently. When you recognize what you're excelling at, this becomes a part of your brand unintentionally as those who take part trust what you say. What are you great at?

WENDY LARSON

BRANDING YOURSELF

It's not a secret anymore that network marketing is climbing in popularity and supporting people from all over the world as a reputable source of income. It is paying off credit card debt and student loans. It is providing ways for new home purchases and adoptions. It is increasing cash flow and making dreams come true. And it's not a secret anymore that social media has become the network marketing platform that leads to digital sales. You can probably identify several network marketers in your feed alone through "how-to" tutorials and difference-making side-by-side photos and don't forget stories of life-changing testimonials. In fact, sales have become such a regular part of social media there really is no escaping it. Sponsored ads. Ads suggested for you. It's all there for you, the consumer, to become enticed by something that somebody wants you to buy. And I would bet that you have absolutely purchased something because it was an ad in your newsfeed—a curling iron, a planner, or even a pro-tip training guru. But here you are. With your product. With your company. And wondering, "Where do I start? How can I compete?"

How do you set yourself apart in a way that will make you more appealing to your audience? How do you market something you love that won't receive the "scroll by"? How do you put yourself out there without "being salesly"? How do you identify what your "brand" is? What is a brand?

First let me share with you a story of my friend, Sandra. Sandra is a housewife, a mother, and a homeschool mom to four kids. She is also a small business owner of a family-owned resort on a lake in Minnesota. People are drawn to her because she is energetic, kind, and funny and makes people feel valued in her posture and her words. She communicates regularly with her social media audience. She is always wishing someone a happy birthday or congratulations on a recent life achievement. She shares live videos weekly on healthy eating habits and provides recipes for people to try. She has a Facebook group which she moderates that is all about natural health tips. Just because. She is engaging. One day she is introduced to a network marketing company that she loves and decides to make this a career. When she starts sharing, people are immediately interested. In fact, Sandra doesn't even have a testimony herself yet and people are interested. In less than two years she has climbed to one of the top ranks of the company? How did she do that?

She did it by branding herself. And it wasn't her company or her products that were her brand. People are saying yes to HER before they even knew what they were saying yes to. She has built a bridge of trust with her online audience years before she offered a single product for sale—this is what makes her significant to her success.

IDENTIFY YOUR STRENGTHS

Strengths. Yes, you have them. I promise. And we are going to identify them. Your strengths are your magnet features. Your strengths are your confidence-building power tools. Your strengths are what you offer to others effortlessly. They are what people love about you and why they are attracted to you. Your strength is a service, and it is going to be used for good! And you have them. I promise. You have "power tools" about you that encourage others to see themselves as you. Sandra has many strengths. In fact, they are endless to someone who might know her as personally as I do. But when it comes to branding herself, her strengths are like an unwritten billboard. They sell her. And people "buy-in" to what she is offering.

Sandra loves cooking. She loves nutrition and learning about foods and how they nourish our bodies. That intrigue has led to an output of sharing the things she loves about food and cooking. She teaches us about unique superfoods and power nutrients. She shares what it is like trying a new recipe or sharing one that is tried-and-true. People value what she shares because they feel empowered to make better eating choices or cooking something they never thought to before. This is an example of her "brand." Her brand in this particular example is "Cook".

What do you have that you can offer people that costs you nothing? That is the question. Is it cooking, like Sandra? Is it nursing? Or marriage advice? Is it a ministry? Or is it parenting? Is it organizing? Or graphic design? Did you notice that I didn't list things like encourager, peacemaker, hard worker, or activator? Yes, those are all great qualities, and they are important make-up factors. But they aren't your brand. Your brand makes you a billboard for something that you're known for. It is a pillar on which you stand. They would be the things people would describe about you. They might already be listed on your social media page as your description, and this description is your billboard for what you offer people. Can you identify 3-5 things about yourself that you feel could identify you from an attraction marketing aspect?

DEFINE WHAT YOUR BRAND IS

Okay, I think we are getting in a groove now, starting to get a feel for what we are looking for, a feel for what we are not. When I first studied branding, I have to admit, I felt like I was a lot of things and struggled to narrow down what I wanted my platform to become.

"Your brand is what people say about you when you're not in the room."
Rebekah Fowlkes.

I needed to look at myself from the eyes of the viewer, the customer, and/or the prospect. What did they see when they looked at me? If I am talking about how unhealthy I am and trying to market a wellness product, who is buying that? Wouldn't that be confusing? Who was I? And was I consistent in it? Insecurities will naturally creep in when we define who we are to our social audience. We think we have to show people what we think they want to see. Not true. They want to see the real us, not somebody we are not . . .

- A happily married couple (fail)
- An artsy, crafty homeschool mom (hair is getting pulled out)
- A gut health guru (with daily stomach aches)

While all of these are certainly solid branding pillars, are they you? Authenticity sells more than anything because it builds a bridge from the consumer to the brand. Trust me—people know when you aren't authentic. You can't sell something you aren't confident in. And I am not talking about confidence in your product. I am talking about confidence in your brand: YOU.

Let me share with you my personal experience with defining my brand. Remember how I said that I felt like I was a lot of things? It's true! I am! However, when I think about my ideal prospect, it instantly narrows down those with whom I will identify myself with branding. You see, my message needs to be clear. It can't be a whole bunch of things, because then I am speaking to a whole bunch of people, and I don't want to speak to a whole bunch of people. I don't need their sales. I need their buy-in because that is staying power. That is my trust factor. When I was defining my personal brand, I narrowed it down to all things "home-related" because my ideal customer was also a woman who was looking for solutions in her home. Homeschooling, homemaking, homesteading, and homeopathy—I stick to these pillars and my message is clear. If I can relate to the ideal prospect in these areas, then my product will also be something that she needs, and when the time arises, we discuss it. She bought into me long before she bought into my product. I help her feel like she is already winning in her own corner with homeschooling, homemaking, and homesteading, so when we talk about homeopathy, she is already confident in her decisions. I have a customer for life because I have bridged the gap between us, and we have relatable experiences together. I am confident in my brand because it is authentically me . . . in my strengths.

KNOWING YOUR TARGET AUDIENCE

See how we are building one experience of branding right on top of the next? Now that you are narrowing down your endless list of wonderful character traits and strengths, we are going to help you do so even more by knowing your target audience. This is actually fun. You can build your own "avatar," so to speak, which is going to give you one person. Yes, you heard me. One. My friend Kari Hafeli always says, "When you're talking to everybody, you're talking to nobody," and it is so true. I want to speak directly to the heart of my ideal customer. How do I find them? First of all, let's look at our social media presence. Who is liking our posts? Engaging in our stories? Commenting on our writings? This is not to make you feel like you have to compare yourself to anybody. It's actually the opposite. This will help you see if your ideal customer is the one who is actually engaging with you. Because this is who we want to be talking to. Now that you've identified that, we can move on to building your perfect "avatar," because you will be coming back to look at this again once you've created your ideal customer.

- What is their name?
- What is their age?
- What is their job/career?

- What do they value most?
- What are their hobbies?
- Where do they live?
- What are their likes/dislikes?
- What do they drive?
- What is their home like?
- What is their lifestyle like?
- What brands do they like?
- Get to know them.

Did you write these answers down? Did you come up with a whole new person? Can you trust yourself enough to know that this person is your target audience and stop trying to speak to everybody? Yes, we know your product IS for everybody. But it is you that has the "yes factor," not your product. Speaking directly to the heart and life of your ideal customer because you are authentically you will build that bridge of trust. This is what we want. When I began to create my own personal "avatar," I actually created a vision board of who she was, a work-at-home-career woman named Leslie. She is in her early 40s and likes nice things. She drives a nice car. She has a beautiful house and gorgeous flower gardens. Her children are homeschooled, and she longs to have her home in order. She just needs to know where to begin. She works hard, loves cozy spaces, and enjoys lots of family time. I feel now that I have a real person to connect with—she has become my target audience. I am speaking to all the "Leslies" out there.

BE CONSISTENT

Practice what you are learning through consistent attempts. When you are building your brand, you will naturally begin to refine what it is and who you are. Branding yourself is multiple layers of exposure, not just saying it once or twice. It is in your social profile. It is in your business email. It is in your email signature. It is your cover photo. It is your description. It is what people say about you when they talk about you. It is everywhere consistently and the same. It is layered over and over so people can be anywhere and instantly recognize your brand. For example, look at your favorite coffee shop or pizza place. You can identify their logo without words. You can identify their words and not see a logo because they have perfectly practiced multiple exposures and consistency in their branding so that you can know about them without seeing it. Or see them and know their catchphrase. You are a business, just like any other business. And what makes network marketing unique is that YOU are the brand, not your company. Your company already has its brand. People might like what your company is, but it is really you who they are saying yes to.

My challenge for you is to go through all of your accounts and identify if your brand is consistent with what you are putting out there. Level up!

I am at the top of my own company and just now realizing how very important it is to be consistent with my brand. I didn't pay attention to it before. Seven to ten years ago we didn't have the same access to social media platforms as we do now. My brand was consistently doing community education courses and showing people what I knew about health and cooking. Times are changing.

Every day we compete with every other company out there in the digital sales world. Our lack of showing up is providing someone else a straight shot of marketing to our ideal customer. And they will consume whatever they are attracted to because it is a layered exposure.

MOMENTUM MAKERS

1. **IDENTIFY YOUR STRENGTHS.** Who are we to our community of influence that allows us to serve in authenticity? It can be our deepest passions. It can be something personal. It can be something that adds value to our customers and helps them feel relatable to us.
2. **DEFINE YOUR BRAND.** What are your 3-5pillars of identity? Remember, we know you are a lot of amazing things, but who are you known for? Keep it simple yet impacting. Is it authentic?
3. **DISCOVER YOUR IDEAL CUSTOMER.** "When you're talking to everybody, you're talking to nobody." Use the questions above to write out your ideal customer and envision that you are speaking right to them. Know them personally. They will become a natural selection process for your product. They are already bought in.
4. **BE CONSISTENT.** "If you want to grow up, you need to show up." This is a pretty common saying in the network marketing world, and it covers a multitude of areas in which we redefine ourselves. Be certain that you are practicing layered exposures of branding yourself on every platform that you use. Is your message clear? Is it consistent? Does it flow naturally from platform to platform so your viewers see the same thing?
5. **BUILDING YOUR BRAND CAN BE FUN!** And it really allows for creative energy to flow. Try not to overthink anything, because when you are authentically yourself and operating in your strengths, people are naturally attracted to you. They are relating to the real you. The real you is magnificent. You have so many things that add value to others. Your brand is what people say "yes" to. Remember that. You already have the yes power to whatever it is you are selling. It is YOU.

TORSTEN SEDLMEIER

FROM BEING A "NO NAME" TO A "NAME" WITH SOCIAL MEDIA BRANDING

HOW IT ALL STARTED

When I discovered network marketing over 30 years ago, this business model was completely unknown to me, and I didn't know what to do to be successful. However, I recognized the potential and implemented exactly what my upline taught me and was unsuccessful because I was just the "guinea pig" for their new ideas.

So I decided to read books about network marketing, go to seminars, talk to really successful people in this industry, and then apply what I had learned accordingly. I put everything I learned into practice and found that there were things that really work and things that didn't work for me at all. I taught my team all of the things that I've had success with because I didn't want anyone on my team to suffer as I did and I wanted all of my team members to be successful from the start.

My philosophy has always been to build a large and profitable but also a sustainable and long-lasting business through a satisfied customer base, "raving fans of the products or services," as well as helping many people in my team to earn hundreds or thousands of dollars every month from it. Of course, everyone who starts with network marketing wishes this, but not everyone will succeed. Sometimes it's up to you; sometimes it's due to circumstances you can't control.

I've had my "ups and downs" in this industry. It took me eight years to make it to the top of my first network, and when I left the company, I slipped into financial ruin. I was forced to take an additional job, and we had no heating for two winters and went to the food bank to get food. At night I even collected bottles and cans from trash cans to recycle to pay the bills.

Anyone who knows my story knows that I have never lost my faith in network marketing. After a new opportunity arose with a new company, I took it, and in a very short time I was in the highest career level, and after only two years, I was qualified as the fastest partner in the "Million Dollar Club." What was the secret of my extraordinary success?

FROM "NO NAME" TO A "NAME" BY BRANDING YOURSELF

In the beginning, it is of course important to acquire knowledge on how to work successfully in network marketing. Today there are countless possibilities for this, including training courses, books, videos, YouTube videos, and online seminars, etc. Find a coach and mentor who is where you would like to go and who has already proven success. However, in the next step, it is essential to implement what you have learned.

You will find that there are basic principles in network marketing that have remained unchanged for decades and will never change. You should learn these in order to have long-lasting success in network marketing. I was lucky to learn these basic principles by legends like Mr. Jim Rohn, Tony Robbins and other top trainers who trained me personally. However, what changes over and over again are systems and technologies. It is important, especially in times when social media and branding are becoming more and more important to success, to be adaptable and to be open to breaking new ground. What still works today and is "in" may be "out" tomorrow.

Facebook, Instagram & Co., and ZOOM online seminars, etc. didn't even exist a few years ago, but I was open to learning everything about them. Over the years, I've gotten better and better at them, and what used to be offline has moved more and more online. Today 90% of my business is online via the Internet. This is how I built now-a-days teams of 50,000+ internationally and got recognized in the "Million Dolllar Club"—from being literally broke before, collecting bottles and cans from trash cans, and getting food from the food bank for the family. Yes, by following and teaching these principles and strategies, 80% of my leaders who never have been in network marketing or never have been successful in this industry before, are breaking records now.

It is important to build your own brand by conveying values and attracting people with whom you would like to work in a team. Ask yourself, "What do I stand for, what do I want to be known for, what values are important to me and I want to convey, what should my followers think of when they hear my name?" It is important to be yourself and not just copy someone else. Be yourself, with your whole being and the characteristics that define you as a person. You will attract the people who suit you and who are also fun to work with. To do this, define your target group, which people you want to address in which area.

Next, find the appropriate media or media that you want to use to market yourself and your brand. Ideally, you use two or three platforms so you don't get bogged down. Whether it's Facebook, LinkedIn, Tik-Tok, Instagram, Twitter, podcasts, or Clubhouse, follow people who are where you want to go and get ideas, tips, and suggestions that you can implement on your profiles without completely copying their contents. You have to be yourself. You have to become your own brand. You have to market yourself as a person, as a brand.

THE IMPORTANCE OF BRINGING VALUE TO YOUR FOLLOWER

One of the most important basic principles in social media marketing is to give first; that is, to convey values, and to build relationships before you "take"—to win people over to your cause. The biggest mistake a beginner can make is becoming a "Spamela Anderson"; never blurt it straight out and offer your product or service without any relationship building. This will always fail in the long run, and if people on your team duplicate this as well, you create self-made problems that do not create lasting success and contribute to the fact that your company, your product, or your service (no matter how good they are) get a negative touch that is very difficult to remove.

If you want to be successful in social media branding, you have to actually be social. If one of your followers mentions you in a tweet, respond. If someone asks a question on your Facebook page, answer them. If someone comments on your Instagram post, comment back. If you answer questions to consolidate your expert status and not only show goodwill, you become more approachable and can present your knowledge. In addition, you automatically build more and more trust. It is important not to spam your answers or to appear keen to sell. Your goal is first and foremost to consolidate your personal brand and your status and only then to sell something.

Therefore: give, give, give, and convey value, create trust, build relationships . . . and ONLY THEN offer your product or service.

I learned all this when I became a member of the "Next Level Mastermind Group" with Eric Worre and a member of Frazer Brookes "Inner Circle." We learn and share the latest ideas and strategies, especially what is and isn't working on social media. So, in order to succeed and improve yourself on social media, look for good books, like this one in your hands, and good trainings, coaches and mentors!

GET FOLLOWERS ON SOCIAL MEDIA AND INCREASE YOUR REACH

Your "capital" in social media marketing is the number of your active followers who follow, like, share, comment on your posts, and over time, become fans of you. Of course, this won't happen overnight and needs patience, perseverance, and consistency. Invest time DAILY for postings in the various platforms that you use.

How do you get new followers and increase your reach? There are, of course, many different ways of doing this, and it depends on the different platforms. But here, too, caution is advised: the providers change their algorithms at irregular intervals; i.e. what has worked today may only work to a limited extent or not at all tomorrow. That is why it is particularly important here to look for appropriate social media professionals who are always up to date so you can take part in appropriate training courses to be able to react quickly to changes and gain a competitive advantage over competitors. Nothing changes as quickly as online algorithms.

I use my private profile on Facebook to get to know new people and build relationships. I try to make acquaintances from strangers who interact with me and then become Facebook friends or Instagram followers. By building relationships I try to create friendships out of it. Some of these friendships turn into customers or business partners over time, and ideally, life-long friendships emerge from them.

I met my friend Steve from the UK over 10 years ago online. For two years we kept in contact online and exchanged ideas, and an online friendship developed. When I changed companies and informed Steve about it, he showed interest. We met for the first time in Amsterdam at the airport hotel. It was such a warm encounter that when we were asked how long we'd known each other, the attendees couldn't imagine that it was our first live encounter. Over the last two years, we had built up such a close trust-base online that a real friendship developed out of it. Steve decided to start on my team and choose me as a mentor and coach and became my best student. At the same time, this former online friendship turned into such a close friendship that today we see ourselves as a family, as "brothers from another mother." He became not only a top leader and important part in my organization, but he is now teaching other people in our industry how to become successful by building over social media.

YOUR PROFILE IS YOUR BUSINESS CARD—YOUR REACH YOUR POTENTIAL

Your profile on Facebook or other platforms is your business card, and your visitors get a first impression of you and whether or not they might want to work with you one day. It is, first of all, important to have a positive image of yourself on all social media channels, including an appealing profile picture as well as positive content on your page. It is best to use the same profile pictures uniformly on the various online portals so that your followers immediately have a recognition feature. Inconsistent branding is confusing. Your target audience wants to experience your brand the same way, no matter where. A messy brand on social media harms your overall branding, brand awareness, engagement, and ultimately your sales. Your pictures should come across as positive and be of good quality. You might even invest a small amount in order to have the photos taken by a professional.

Professional tip: Always keep yourself strictly neutral when it comes to topics such as religion, politics, sports, world events, etc., and always convey a positive, sympathetic, and friendly attitude. It may be necessary for you to make a Facebook clean up, i.e. to analyze your postings retrospectively and, if necessary, to delete them. Why is this so important? Imagine you are a fan of a soccer team and you keep posting something about that team but a potential customer is a fan of another team and hates your team. It stands to reason that you probably won't become too close as Facebook friends because of this one thing, and it may even break the foundation of one day working together. When it comes to certain topics, neutrality is a must in social media branding.

Look for 3-5 topics that interest you and with which you can identify that distinguish you as a person or belong to you and about which you can publish a post every week. It can be a hobby, such as cooking, riding a bike, or drawing, or it can be your pet or traveling, etc. Once a week you do a Facebook LIVE, once a week a post about your product or service, and a post in your feed on one of these topics every day for the rest of the week. Make sure that you share this post in your Facebook stories. If you also use Instagram, upload this post and the story separately to Instagram, which in turn can have a positive effect on your algorithm.

Professional tip: Before you publish your post on Facebook, "heat up" your Facebook algorithm to increase your reach because your Facebook post is only displayed to a fraction of your Facebook friends. However, if you interact with friends on a daily basis, leave happy birthday greetings or life events, especially 5-10 minutes before you publish your post, it will be visible to more people. Instead of the "like" button, be sure to use one of the other symbols and comment on your friends' contributions. After you've posted your post, interact with other friends again for 5-10 minutes, which will increase your reach again. The more people who liked and commented on your post in the first 10 minutes determines how many other people your post will be shown to in your friends' list, as Facebook "thinks" that if so many people react, the post must be important.

Basically, "Facebook LIVES" and uploaded videos are shown to more people than images that you upload. Do not link videos to other platforms (YouTube, Vimeo, etc.), because Facebook of course does not want you to generate traffic on other platforms via Facebook, which will massively limit your reach.

Professional tip: If you have hardly any reach and are just starting out with social media branding, you can use "Facebook LIVE" to greatly increase your reach in a relatively short period of time by doing one "Facebook LIVE" DAILY for at least 30 days. Don't get frustrated if at first you're low on viewers; this will change over time. Encourage your audience to interact by asking them, for example, which city they are from or whether they are watching live or the replay or ask for their opinion on what you have just said, etc.

I know it takes a bit of effort to go LIVE on the air and to go through it every day. A few years ago, my sweetheart was very discreet on social media, and I encouraged her to step over her shadow and do more on social media. From tentative beginnings, her social media reach grew and she got more and more followers in her field and an ever-greater degree of awareness. So she ventured to other platforms such as TikTok and YouTube. Today some of her posts and videos have not just thousands but tens of thousands of views, and her best video has over 1.2 million views.

I am repeatedly asked how to increase your reach on Facebook and other platforms when you have few followers and friends. My recommendation is to look for groups that cover your interests or your three to five topics. If you are interested in cooking and recipes, go to the appropriate groups and subscribe to them. Maybe you are a single mother—join a group in which single mothers share ideas. Or if you are interested in mountain biking, look for a suitable group. Bring added value to your groups without talking about your business, your product, or your service (no spam!). Like and comment on other peoples' posts. You may find an article, a picture, or something else that adds value to the group—post this to the group. If you notice people in the group who you find likeable and with whom you would like to talk about your product or service later, make a friend request outside of the group. If this is accepted, first develop a relationship with the person. Interact with this person and wait; if you are approached because of your postings or after a certain amount of time, ask appropriate questions that will lead to your conversation about your product or business. And the same applies here: learning by doing.

Another tip to increase the reach on Facebook or Instagram is to use hashtags. Find hashtags that fit your post or your topic. If someone searches for the relevant topic, you can be found through it. The principle here is not to exaggerate the number of hashtags; currently, up to 10 hashtags per post is optimal. You can vary the hashtags on a daily basis, but they should match the relevant post.

Create content that people enjoy sharing. Your content is the foundation of your success on social media, and it needs to get people to click, interact with, and share it. Also, use great pictures—pictures drive the engagement up incredibly. Facebook posts with pictures get 2.3 times more engagement, and tweets with pictures have 150% more retweets than tweets without pictures.

Another way to increase the number of followers and engagement is through competitions and promotions. One possibility would be a raffle for your product or service or a prize of $50 or $100 in cash (via PayPal) or vouchers (Amazon, Apple, etc.). Raffle these off among all people who, for example, share your feed with the raffle on your site or mark five people from their friend's list, etc. This will again increase your reach and visibility and expand your "Circle of Influence" in the ranks of your followers and, in turn, in their follower or friends lists. In addition, the marked people receive a notification from Facebook or Instagram that they have been marked in a post by a friend, and since most people are curious, they also look at your post or even take part in your raffle. Or they'll find your profile appealing and follow you.

Those who do not move with the times will be moved by the times, and those who do not promote will "die" in the online business. But don't be shocked that 20-30 percent of the people who follow you because of raffles will unfollow you after the promotion is over. However, if you have an interesting and engaging profile, 70-80 percent of people stay. It is worth thinking long-term, gradually increasing your online presence with patience, perseverance, and consistency, and marketing yourself as an independent brand.

MOMENTUM MAKERS

1. **ALWAYS BE YOURSELF—NEVER BE SOMEONE ELSE.** There are always people who are more beautiful, younger, more attractive, more intelligent, or more successful, and there is no point in taking on a role to please others. If you are authentic, you will attract the very people who like and love you for who you are because they can identify with you.

2. **YOUR PROFILE ON SOCIAL MEDIA IS YOUR BUSINESS CARD, YOUR BRAND.** If you want successful branding on social media, make it consistent and use two to three platforms on which you interact and share valuable content on a daily basis.

3. **BE SOCIAL.** Social media is a conversation and should be two-way. Interact with your followers, answer questions, be polite, build trust, and become an expert in your niche, in your field, without spamming.

4. **INCREASE YOUR REACH.** Bring valuable content, images, and videos so your followers like and share them and interact with you. Run competitions and promotions, integrate your followers, and reward those who are most active in it.

5. **BE CONSISTENT BUT ALSO PATIENT.** Consistency develops routines and builds momentum. It forms habits that become almost second nature. Leadership guru John Maxwell said, "Small disciplines repeated with consistency everyday lead to great achievements gained slowly over time." Success doesn't happen overnight, especially not in social media branding. Patience, persistence, and strategy are the keys to long-term success. Don't ever let failure stop you from pursuing your dreams.

RACHEL PEKAREK

I DIDN'T SET OUT TO BUILD A BRAND, I JUST WANTED LEADS. PERIOD!

"Hey! Just wanted to reach out to you. Been following you for a long time, and you've taught me so much. I've been thinking it's time for me to jump into a business, and I would LOVE to work with you. Can you send me your link to join? By the way . . . what company are you with again?"

Could you just imagine? This message. Inside of your inbox: each month, each week, and eventually each day.

This is network marketing personal branding done well.

Corporately speaking, branding is a marketing practice in which a company creates a name, logo, symbols, or even a "tribe" as a way to distinguish themselves from competitors.

So how does it work for independent network marketing distributors when you have tens of thousands (or more) other reps in the SAME company vying for prospects, let alone the millions of reps in the MLM industry all striving for market share?

For you, the network marketer, it's really less about a logo or special colors—not in today's landscape. It's about stepping out in your UNIQUE qualities, skills, and abilities that make you different from somebody else. You create a personal brand to stand out, and if can do so well, become the

#1 person your network thinks of when they think of ______. *More on this BLANK in a bit ☺

Excellent personal branding means people consider you an influencer, a thought leader, and what I like to call a MicroCelebrity™. This isn't about become a traditional famous TMZ-esque celebrity while losing your soul AND your privacy. No. This is about creating a tribe of raving fans who buy what you sell, join what you do, and tell everyone about you.

But first, let's back up: I never sought out to really build a brand. I just wanted leads. Period.

After three years of building my business offline and doing every single belly-to-belly approach (leads groups, networking groups, Chamber of Commerce, trade shows, even cold calling leads—YUCK!), I was banging my head against the wall. Plus, as an introvert, I truly began to DESPISE working my business because it was borderline painful.

I was hungry, though. I was determined to make network marketing work.

It was a defining moment in my life when I sat down with a mentor for lunch. His name is David Frey, and I truly believe he changed my trajectory with the advice he gave me that day. You see, I looked up to David. He was older, wiser, and super successful doing things called "webinars." (This was back in 2009—am I dating myself yet?)

"I just don't have enough people to talk to!" I moaned and slunk back in my chair looking to David for a miracle.

He laughed and smirked. And then he said it. Five magical words.

"Rachel, ***you have to start doing videos!***"

He proceeded to tell me he believed it was the best way for me to get in front of new people so they could find me, follow me, and learn more about my opportunity.

I chuckled a bit. Why? Well, in 2021, YouTube seems like the most obvious answer. But guess who was on YouTube back in 2009?

Yup. You guessed it . . . cats.

So off I ran. Me and cats. Making videos. It was a hoot!

I began investing in my education on how to create videos and watched dozens of tutorials since I was not so technologically savvy. After a few months, I really started to get the hang of it.

Not to say it was easy. It. Was. NOT! It was terrifying. Uncomfortable. I was a 24-year-old punk kid with no confidence and no real business success to speak of, and now I was sitting in front of a camera. "What do I talk about? I don't have much to say!" So many lies swirled in my head, but as the Nike saying goes, "Just DO IT!" took over, and I would hit record and upload. Over the next 18 months, I had built up my YouTube channel to over 1,000,000 views and gathered over 10,000 subscribers to my email list.

At 26 years old, I had the opportunity to partner with a newer wellness MLM, and using MicroCelebrity™ branding tactics, I went from network marketing failure to the top female money earner in my company in just 16 months.

Building a personal brand has helped me earn an insane living and lead an awesome team that has done over $150,000,000 in revenue all while personally recruiting over 1200 people on social media alone. And the best part is that you can literally rip off and repeat these tactics for your own business by following a few simple tips.

TIP #1 – PICK A BUCKET

Back in 2010, I took a class with ClickFunnels founder Russell Brunson in which he taught me the phrase, "Pick a niche, get rich!" He was teaching affiliate marketers how to find small genres of interest and market an online product (like an eBook) to that niche of people.

When it comes to personal branding, I cannot emphasize enough how powerful this could be for you.

To make it simple, I train this to my coaching clients and leaders in the form of choosing brand buckets. We find these buckets by brainstorming answers to a series of questions:

- What do you study/research in your spare time when not working your business?
- What topic could you speak about for 30 minutes on a ZOOM with almost no preparation?
- What group of people could you easily connect with based on expertise or things you have in common (ie: stay-at-home parents, English Bulldog owners, garden enthusiasts, Christians)

And the most important questions:

- What do you want to be known for?
- If you could become the #1 person in your network known for (fill in the blank), what would it be?

Ah. We finally found the BLANK (from just a few minutes ago; you're still tracking with me, right)? ☺

There's got to be something you're inherently good at, have experience in, or are passionate bout. Maybe it's homeschooling, barrel racing, Bible study, or entrepreneurship. Maybe you're a part-time football coach or volunteer with children at risk. Maybe you are a novice acrylic painter.

Maybe you just finished your certification in herbology and are fanatical about healing via plants!

Some ideas for possible brand buckets:

- Skincare/beauty
- Art/creative hobbies
- Parenting
- Finances/investing
- Business
- Horses/dogs/pets
- Diet and wellness
- Non-toxic living
- Fitness
- Faith/spirituality
- Online marketing
- Social media marketing
- Network marketing
- Gardening
- Outdoors
- Leadership
- Mindset
- Travel
- Politics
- Other: ___________________

TIP #2 – TEACH AS AN EXPERT

Once you've narrowed down on a solid brand bucket, it's time to teach. You might say, "Rachel, I am not an expert. I don't have a degree in this! I'm just struggling to make a DOLLAR in my MLM. How the heck do you expect me to start teaching?"

I say back to you: It's not about being the expert today. You start by **staying one chapter ahead**. And soon enough you'll become an expert!

Let me explain.

Did you ever see the movie *Catch Me If You Can* with Leonardo DiCaprio? Well, Leo was playing Frank Abagnale, Jr. who worked as a doctor, a lawyer, and as a co-pilot for a major airline . . . all before his 18th birthday. As a master of deception, he was also a brilliant forger a skill that gave him his first real claim to fame: at 17 years old, Frank became the most successful bank robber in the history of the United States.

Frank Abagnale, Jr. was finally caught years after staying one step ahead of the authorities while teaching a sociology class at BYU for the entire semester. The FBI asked, "How in the world did you teach that class? You know nothing about advanced sociology?"

Frank's answer was EVERYTHING. "All I had to do was read one chapter ahead of the students.

See, whether you're going to brand yourself as the "great haircare girl," the "essential oil king," or the best "equine expert," you don't need to know it all to start. You just have to be "one chapter" ahead of your audience.

There is something powerful about the psychology of this. If you happen to know something that somebody else doesn't on a particular topic they are interested in, they automatically assume you to have all the answers. BOOM! Instant influence.

But what does TEACHING have to do with building a personal brand in network marketing?

The best and most viral content is one of three things:

1. Educational
2. Inspirational
3. Entertaining

Think about a top-rated podcast on leadership, a best-selling book on overcoming obstacles, or even your favorite viral food videos from Tasty (a Facebook page that has nearly 100 million followers) by making delicious short recipe tutorials.

Viewers learn something. They feel encouraged. Or they laugh and numb out a bit.

What I love about positioning yourself as a "teacher" of sorts in your brand bucket is that it gives you instant authority. And when you're looking to gain influence in network marketing, until you've hit a good pin rank you can still attract others into your business with your personality, unique ability, and skillset in another niche.

When I look at the 350,000+ followers I've attracted on social media in the last decade, I realize that a lot of it has come from teaching SOMETHING and becoming a prolific content creator. I started badly. I started afraid. I "started from the bottom now I'm here!"

Homework: Make a list of 50 things you can talk about in your brand bucket. Use a tool like AnswerThePublic.com if you get stuck. For example, if your passion is weight loss, you might search "lose weight" on AnswerThePublic. Here are some of the results people are searching for:

- "How to lose weight after pregnancy"

- "How to lose weight without exercise"
- "How to lose weight in 10 days"
- "Which vegetables to eat to lose weight"
- "Will I lose weight eating 1000 calories"

And the list goes on and on and on. Imagine every week going Live on Facebook, recording a podcast, or writing a blog post answering these common questions. After a year you'll have over 50+ pieces of content and you'll begin generating a qualified following of people looking to learn from you.

It's funny. When I started on YouTube in 2009, I actually called myself "The Card Teacher" because at the time I was in a greeting card service MLM. I recorded videos explaining how the service worked, how it was more cost-effective than other methods, how to get referrals using the service, even how the company's compensation plan worked.

I was a pipsqueak kid who ended up becoming a top recruiter, enrolling 2-4 distributors a week JUST from my "teacher" YouTube videos. Most of my recruits were NOT local, and most were twice my age.

I wasn't all that successful, but I was teaching. So I gathered natural influence. And so can you!

Now pick a platform (Facebook, Instagram, TikTok, YouTube, whatever!) and begin teaching. You won't be good right away (unless you're just one in a million, and good for you because you're a unicorn) . . . but the great news is nobody will be watching. By the time you find your voice and build your tribe, your skills will have improved.

Any straggler who happened to have seen you in the beginning will have witnessed your transformation, and it'll be exponentially more inspiring.

TIP #3 – CONNECTION NOT COMMISSION

Repeat after me: Be a good human.

Gone are the days of cold messaging a million people a day, sliding into peoples' DM's like, "Hey girl . . ." Stop. Just stop.

A personal brand is only effective if there's a good human behind it. Even larger corporations are moving to creating or elevating a "face" or character of their brand so that people can CONNECT on a human level. I'm sorry, but nobody wants to follow TESLA. They follow Elon Musk, capiche? It's the PERSON.

You want to begin connecting with people on a daily basis. While there are a million ways to build a brand and following now that you've picked your bucket and are beginning to TEACH, you now have to connect and serve the masses.

Naturally, you want to find the people who would be most interested in your content, your value, and—fingers crossed—your opportunity. One of the easiest ways to do this on Facebook is to join Facebook Groups—not to spam or message people with your website link (No! No! No! BE A GOOD HUMAN! This will get you blocked from the group anyway).

Join the group and add value. Join and find the influencers (positive, active members) in the group and friend request them. Comment on people's posts. Build rapport with the admins. If you added 10 new friends a day 6 days a week from a Facebook group in your brand bucket, you'd have 3,120 new friends after a year.

Some of these friends would you see your Facebook Lives teaching. They might see your Facebook stories on a product offer. And a few will begin to fall in love with everything that you do and who you are. They may start sharing your content and tagging friends in your posts. As you connect and have conversations, you likely will find a PROBLEM you can

SOLVE with your network marketing opportunity, and boom, a prospect is born.

One of my friends and mentors, Frazer Brookes, a generic network marketing trainer (one who previously built massive teams and made millions by the time he was 30 in MLM), says in network marketing, "We turn strangers into friends and friends into family."

A stellar personal brand will do just that.

. . .

There is one pitfall to starting a personal brand from scratch, and that is that it can feel really slow. We get 30 views of a YouTube video and want to quit. But just remember, 30 people fill a classroom. We get 250 views on an Instagram Live and feel so dumb. But just remember, 250 people fill an auditorium.

What people really want more than anything is VALUE and CONSISTENCY. Make a promise to yourself, the future of your business, and your loved ones (who deserve your success story the most) that you will never give up.

I cannot believe that 10+ years later, just by teaching and loving on people I've lived this insane life as a MicroCelebrity™ network marketer. Simply insane. I didn't set out to build a brand; I just wanted leads. And oh me oh my, did that ever work.

MOMENTUM MAKERS

1. **YOU HAVE TO BE BAD BEFORE YOU'RE GOOD AND GOOD BEFORE YOU'RE GREAT.** A personal brand will require you to get outside of your comfort zone and start creating content online. JUST DO IT.
2. **SEEK TO BE KNOWN FOR SOMETHING.** Pick a brand bucket that is something you are passionate about. Ideally, it's a market of people who could use your products, services, or opportunity.
3. **BRAINSTORM CONTENT TOPICS THAT WOULD ADDRESS YOUR FOLLOWING'S BIGGEST QUESTIONS, CONCERNS, PROBLEMS, AND GOALS.** When you have the answer to someone's problem, they will automatically trust you as a source of the solution.
4. **THE BEST CONTENT IS EDUCATIONAL, INSPIRATIONAL, AND/OR ENTERTAINING.** Bonus points if you can be all three, but don't pull a muscle trying to do it. If you're not funny, don't be funny. Just do YOU!
5. **CONNECT WITH PEOPLE.** Comment back when they comment. Thank them for watching. Wish them a happy birthday. Start new conversations with people in your niche. Friend them. Return every email personally. Pick up the phone if they need a friend. Be a good human.

BETHANNY CROUSE

ALIGN WITH A COMPANY THAT HAS YOUR SAME VALUES

My mom was an incredible woman. She was known as a top realtor in our area as well as an extraordinarily successful network marketer. Everywhere we went, she made a friend. I believe I inherited a lot of her personality traits and other skills that taught me to be who I have become today. My dad was more on the quiet side with a warm, gentle heart. He always spoke with compassion, and it seemed he always had the right thing to say. Both of my parents have passed on, but I attribute much of my success to be fundamentally tied to my roots.

Every business is different, and depending on how it is run can determine how it is branded. I have been in several different businesses in my life, and I will share my experiences with how different each was when it came to branding.

I started out at a young age as a professional snowboarder, and I was the brand. Most people in the circuits I competed against knew me. They did not see me as the snowboarding company that sponsored me. I was Bethanny Crouse, the girl to beat when it came to boarder-cross in the Summit County, CO circuit because I rarely placed second.

My husband, Chris, and I went on to start a dog daycare and boarding facility in Breckenridge, Colorado. We worked together and created a cute logo, which was a caricature of our dog at the time. The name of our business was The Dog House, which quickly became a well-known brand for Summit County residents. For many years before we opened our business, residents only had one choice when it came to boarding their dog—a place for their dog to spend the night, but it did not include daycare. When The Dog House opened, word spread quickly how your dog could come and play all day and also the spend the night. This helped our business become a success from day one.

We also owned a coffee kiosk in the entrance of our local grocery store in Breckenridge. We kept it simple and named it The Coffee Cart. The Coffee Cart served Bongo Billie's coffee, which was made with beans from a local roastery. They were known for their fair-trade, organic coffee. Bongo Billie's was the brand of coffee beans, and everyone called The Coffee Cart, Bongo Billie's. Locals knew my husband as "Coffee Chris" because he ran the shop mostly, but they knew him as the owner of Bongo Billie's, even though that was technically not the name of the business. Bongo Billie's was the brand.

Another business I owned was Crouse Contracting. I was a general contractor and would build and sell million-dollar homes in Breckenridge, CO. I had my GC license and a crew that went with me from house to house. We typically only worked on one or two houses at a time. No one even knew the name of my company. When I walked into The Breckenridge Building Center, everyone knew my name. I was Bethanny Crouse, the only female GC in the county, and most of them knew what house I was working on at the time by the name of the street the house was on. When I walked into the Summit County building department, it was the same thing. The receptionists, the inspectors, and the bosses all knew me but not the name of my company.

With only 4,300 full-time residents in Breckenridge at the time, I knew a lot of people because most residents had a dog, drank coffee, or were in construction. I also was a mother to Lilah and Waylan, who were highly active in community activities.

In 2009, I was introduced to an international superfood network marketing company by my best friend, Star Hayward. She knew that I cared a lot about health and fitness. As a matter of fact, she and I first met at a fitness studio. One day she asked if Chris and I would like to complete a health challenge with her and her husband. After looking into the products and the company and doing my own research, I decided we would give the products a try. However, I was clear to let Star know that with three businesses and two toddlers at the time, I was not interested in the business opportunity.

Within five days of using the products, I called Star elated about my results. My "mommy brain" had gone away. The brain fog had lifted. My energy was through the roof, and I was no longer taking naps everyday with Waylan, who was two years old at the time. I went on to lose six pounds and six inches and achieved my ideal shape.

I started shouting the company name from the rooftops. I sent Facebook messages out to all my contacts asking if they had heard of the company. I had a display of empty containers at The Dog House. I began selling the products at The Coffee Cart. My car had the company logo on it. Even my snowboard had a huge logo sticker. I quickly began branding the company name everywhere, however I could get the word out that these products were amazing!

I am a woman who prioritizes clean eating, longevity, healthy solutions, exercise, philanthropy, ethically sourced products, and sustainability. So when I found a company that already prioritized these same values, it was a match made in heaven. I knew that aligning with a company that had a trusted brand built from day one was like a joint venture already set up for me.

Somehow and some way, I did enroll a lot of product users. (Probably because I was pushy.) I became a sponsor monster. I won every trip the company offered due to my high enrollments. I was awarded and recognized as one of the top three enrollers in the entire company in 2011, even though I was only working the business in the pockets of my life. I mostly sent messages on Facebook whenever I was at The Dog House, running the office.

By my third year of sharing the superfood products that changed my health, I had received a 1099 for $81,000. I looked at my husband in amazement. How could this possibly be? Sharing products that I loved on Facebook by spamming messages, I had not only earned enough money to pay for my products that year (which was my only goal), but I was close to achieving a six-figure income all while helping people achieve better health, which I LOVED! I had become a personal trainer at the age of 18 because I was so into health & fitness but never followed through with that as a career after the age of 22 simply because I moved onto growing businesses that I thought would give me time freedom.

Aligning with my network marketing company made sense. I had found my passion. Years earlier, I had begun strengthening my authentic self through personal development, and this company seemed like an extension to that. It would allow me to continue to grow as a person while helping others do the same.

We decided to sell our businesses to see what would happen if I focused on network marketing truly as a business opportunity. We were able to sell the two businesses with the well-known brands, of course—The Dog House and The Coffee Cart both sold within the first six months of us listing them. Because Crouse Contracting was not known as a brand, I decided to dissolve it. This was during a tough economic time anyway to build houses, so it made the most sense, and I never looked back.

The next chapter of our lives had begun. After seventeen years, we left the snowy winters in Breckenridge and began living six months on the island of Kaua'i, where we had honeymooned and lived back in 1999. My husband home schooled Lilah and Waylan, which allowed me focused time to build my network marketing business. After all, we decided together that this would be an opportunity to create a legacy income for our kids and many generations to come since the income I was able to create would be willable.

Although this was the year that I went "full time" as a professional network marketer, there were also a lot of distractions. The beach was my biggest distraction of all! I loved to surf, stand-up paddleboard, snorkel with the turtles, and hunt for shells. I constantly was asking Chris and the kids if they were done school so we could go to the beach. I began living my life out loud on social media. I was hardly working and doing a whole lot of playing. I've always felt as if everything happens for a reason!

Network marketing allowed me to sell my businesses and create a life of time and financial freedom. When I did, I became the brand. Living six months on Kaua'i and six months in Breckenridge, CO caused people to notice. I was surfing, hiking, snorkeling, snowboarding, camping, SUP-ing, and shell collecting … living a life that others wanted. Without even knowing it, I was using something called "attraction marketing" to network and create curiosity.

Even though I was not consciously working as much as I had anticipated when I sold my businesses, my network marketing business continued to grow due to living my life out loud. I was attracting more people online who wanted to do the business versus product users, and some of them were already my clients.

A couple I met while working out at the same fitness studio where I also met Star Hayward became clients of mine early on in my network marketing journey. Laura had just had her third son, and the weight was not coming off as easily as it did with the first two. She reached out to me because she wanted to implement the products for her post-partum weight loss journey. Scott had begun teaching classes at the very same fitness studio where we had all met, and he began using the sports performance line of products that my company offered. Although they had two different goals, they had achieved the results they were each looking for and became confident in the products.

They later became successful entrepreneurs in the fitness industry, owning three gyms in Denver, CO. They joke that they were closet users of our company's products for over four years. They thought network marketing was taboo, so they were very hesitant to share what they were doing with others.

They watched as Chris and I lived our lives between Kaua'i and Colorado. They were sick of the snow themselves, and Laura dreamt of living at the beach. Scott worked exceptionally long hours training all their clients. He rarely had time to spend with Laura and their three boys. That is when a lightbulb went off for Laura.

Network marketing is simply word-of-mouth marketing. It's the best way to get the word out and to share things you love with those you love. They grew their gyms from one location to three, using all word-of-mouth marketing. Why couldn't they do the same with these superfood products? If one of their clients had great results, they would tell others what they were using and regardless of who got them started; Laura and Scott would benefit financially because our compensation plan does not have levels. We are very blessed that it pays to infinity and it worked in their favor. Not only did they earn a passive income, but their clients were now putting the best nutrition in their bodies!

The way I was living my life out loud on social media inspired them to look more deeply at the business opportunity with our company. They have since gone on to become two of the top leaders within my organization.

On the other hand, I was not doing so well branding myself when it came to in-person encounters. I met someone who I inspired greatly and later came to find out she joined an entirely different company.

While living six months on Kaua'i, I did my best to network and make friends. I will never forget a girl named Sarah who I met at a meetup. She was very into health & wellness, but she was working a corporate career and was very unhappy. She talked about wanting to find something that would give her time and financial freedom, something she could do from home. She was the perfect potential business partner for me because what she was describing was exactly what I had found.

I sold my businesses to become a network marketer and to create time and financial freedom in my life, which was exactly what she desired. She simply thought that I sold products, and she was not interested in selling.

After I moved off island, Sarah called me and asked if I remembered her. Of course I remembered her. When we met, she had described a dream life that I was living. She went on to tell me how after I moved away, she began following me on social media and decided to join a network marketing company. She saw the profession as an opportunity, and she had become so successful that she was asked to share her story on stage. In her story, it began with me and how I inspired her to make a change and to join the profession of network marketing. Although I was flattered and excited for her, I also felt deflated.

It was at that very moment that I realized my posture needed to change. I thought back to the pro-snowboarder I was and the general contractor I was. Everyone knew me as me. I was the girl who always took first place in boarder-cross. I was the only female general contractor who built incredible homes that everyone admired. I needed to be that person in my new career. I had only shared the products with Sarah. I hadn't told her what I could offer if she partnered with me and my company.

I stepped back from my sponsor monster role and I stepped into leadership—teaching others my proven systems and how to dream big and to design the life that they want all while putting superior superfood nutrition in their bodies and helping others do the same! It was only fitting that my network marketing company evolved as well. They established an incredible Leader-In-Action formula, which I began to follow. It was not just about what I was doing on my own—it was more about who I was helping along the way. Most importantly, the life I was living became my brand and the company was my vehicle.

I stopped sharing the company name all over my social media and began intentionally sharing it in other ways, mainly by listening to people when I met them. They would typically share with me why they needed these superfood products.

Everyone is so consumed about building a brand by sharing who they are, what they look like, if their timeline is aesthetically pleasing, and if they are using the right filter. What is most important, in my mind, is sharing your authentic message, your transparency, vulnerability, your conscious alignment, and the value that you bring, as well as finding a company that aligns with your same values.

I recognized that I could align my personal values and ideas to support the magnificent brand already in place by the company, a company that had products that would change the way I feel and look every day. I did not have to recreate the existing brand. I simply had to align with it. I looked at my values of supporting my best health in an environment that was collaborative instead of competitive, an environment centered around a culture of contribution with a focus on ethical sourcing and sustainability.

I got to work on sharing my story and my experience. I utilized systems already in place and created some of my own. My personal brand, Livin' & Givin', has become an extension of this multi-billion dollar international health and wellness company. Livin' & Givin' is a lifestyle brand for people who have chosen to partner with me. We are all about Livin' life to the fullest and Givin' back in every way that we can.

People who were watching me knew that my priorities centered around exercise, mindful eating habits, good nutritional choices, time freedom, and being present with my family. They also saw me supporting other people in finding their financial success so that together we could impact the world with positive change.

Sometimes a brand must be curated from scratch, just as it was when I started The Dog House and The Coffee Cart. I had built systems and started a company all on my own. However, sometimes it can be much easier than that. When you align with a company that matches your values and priorities, it is basically plug and play. Your message continues to support your integrity. Your brand becomes synonymous with what you represent, and together everyone wins. When you can find a leader or a mentor within that same company who appreciates and encourages everyone's unique abilities, that is the cherry on top of the cake.

MOMENTUM MAKERS

1. **ALIGN WITH A COMPANY THAT ALREADY HAS A TRUSTED BRAND THAT ALIGNS WITH YOUR CORE VALUES.** Find a company that already prioritizes your same values, and it will be a match made in heaven. Aligning with a company that has a trusted brand built from day one is like a joint venture already set up for you.
2. **PARTNER WITH A LEADER OR MENTOR WHO HAS ALREADY ACHIEVED THE SUCCESS YOU ARE LOOKING FOR AND HAS SYSTEMS IN PLACE.** When you can find a leader or a mentor within your same company who appreciates and encourages everyone's unique abilities, that is the cherry on top of the cake.
3. **INSPIRE OTHERS TO BECOME THE BEST VERSION OF THEMSELVES AND TO LIVE THE LIFE THAT THEY DESIRE.** Network marketing is simply word-of-mouth marketing. It's the best way to get the word out and to share things you love with those you love.
4. **PEOPLE WILL RELATE MUCH MORE TO YOUR STRUGGLES THAN THEY WILL YOUR TRIUMPHS.** Be you. Be real. Be vulnerable.
5. **DO NOT TRY TO BE PERFECT.** Go live in your robe with bed head. This shows people the real, authentic you, and most people will relate.

MOMENTUM MAKERS

6. **DO NOT SPAM MESSAGES TO PEOPLE ASKING THEM IF THEY WANT TO JOIN YOUR TEAM.** Don't be pushy, but live your life—people are watching you, so get to work on sharing your story and your experiences, and the life you are living will become your brand and the company will be your vehicle.

RIKKI JAMES

FIND YOUR SPARK AND YOUR BRAND WILL FOLLOW

When I started my business, I only had 52 Facebook friends and an anonymous FB name. I was only on social media to stay in contact with a few like-minded people after a previous online forum I was a part of abruptly dissolved.

Not only did I have ZERO interest in starting a real online presence, but also I was actually turned off by the whole idea. To me, social media always seemed either very fake/picture-perfect OR was full of people spilling way too many unnecessary details about their lives.

I don't want to see how your two-year-old-already knows all his shapes, colors, letters, sign language, Japanese, AND Latin. Or your overly filtered, photoshopped, and unrealistic but somehow also supposed to be "spontaneous" family picture of everyone in matching pajamas making cupcakes in your flawless kitchen. Just no.

I really don't need to know that your boyfriend cheated on you *again* or that your gout is flaring. I sure don't want to see your kid's turd during potty training, every single meal you've eaten this week, or each time you've completed your workout. I see enough unsolicited turds on my own parenting adventure, thank you very much.

There's a super thin line between being REAL and airing your dirty and embarrassing laundry for everyone to see. Or between inspiring people in areas of your life vs. sharing way too many superfluous details and turning people off.

It's tough to figure out how to boldly share your talents, wisdom, and successes and not come across as a know-it-all or inauthentic or that your success is unattainable.

I wasn't sure I was going to be able to stay on the right side of this line!

I stepped into the social media scene very hesitantly. I have always been a bit unorthodox and never quite fit in at my local park's playdates. At the time, I had five children (now we have seven!), we homeschool, traveled full-time, used alternative methods for healing, worked from home, and had abundance and positive mindsets. Nothing about our lives has ever been conventional.

Conventional or not, I knew I had to learn social media in order to be successful in my business. I also had a deep desire to transform lives and empower families to rebel against the norm and take back their power. America is the land of the free, with endless possibilities and one of the most advanced medical industries in the world. But I saw more and more people struggling in every way. Fifty-four percent of our children are on prescription meds; this is the first generation where the parents are expected to outlive the children!

So many people are stuck in jobs that aren't fulfilling and living lives that are uninspired. Poverty/negative mindset has become acceptable and are the new normal.

I was so excited to show people how powerful they were and what they are capable of—to help inspire how to keep your power and stop giving it away so freely. I could not wait to share how to think outside the box, to question everything and teach how to trust your intuition.

I knew social media would give me the platform to do this!

Would I be able to be authentic AND grow my social media? Would I be able to juggle my family life and also keep some sense of privacy if I built this?

I quickly realized that not only could I be genuine in my online presence, but it was also the act of sharing genuinely that ended up being the key to my success!

This would be my first tip. **Be authentic. Be YOU. Find your passion and build your brand around it!**

As I started sharing my passions in a bold and unfiltered manner, my online community organically (and rapidly) grew. Within 18 months I grew from 50 friends to a team of thousands and a six-figure income.

I started sharing all of the alternative remedies we used on a normal basis; I shared my home births, how we traveled so often with such a large family, homeschooling tips, goofy family stories, gentle parenting concepts, and fun conspiracy theories. When one of my children had a serious burn, I shared what we did to quickly help the pain and naturally address it. When another kiddo had a raging fever, I showed step-by-step our favorite remedies. Healing eyesight and avoiding glasses? We did it and showed how.

My posts were shared more and more, and I became a page people could come to in search of holistic health and all thing unconventional.

The more I shared all the things that made us unconventional, the more successful I became. Which is my next tip! **Find something unique about yourself or your family and get good at sharing it.** I find it incredibly inspiring that there are SO MANY successful people in this business, and they each have their own unique gifts.

What kept me lonely in my small town is what made me successful online. The world NEEDS your gifts! It needs your inspiration and wisdom! And you have unlimited amounts of it; you just have to tap in and access it.

Third tip: **CARE ABOUT PEOPLE!** The more I cared about my fellow man and their well-being, the more my business flourished. People knew I was a safe space. I was genuine and tried my hardest to answer every message I received, even when that grew to dozens of messages a day. I fell in love with empowering others. It became my calling, and it no longer mattered if I fit in at my local park! I found true friends all over the world! When you find a niche that adds value to the lives of others, loyalty usually follows. In network marketing, fewer things are as important as retention. People want to be a part of something bigger, so creating an environment of genuine care and trust makes your community SOLID.

My "brand" came along by accident, and after three years into my social media journey, I launched my blog. I was already earning six figures in one of the top levels of my company, but my influence (even outside of my own team) was growing rapidly, and I needed to streamline my information in order to help more people. I knew there was a better way to get my information out there—all in one place instead of having to spend so much time answering all of the personal messages. (Work smarter, not harder!) It is still an absolute dream come true to be able to make the amount of money I do while helping other people. It is extremely fulfilling to have become so successful just by sharing my gifts with others!

My blog and brand are a representation of who I truly am. I did things a bit backward. I had no clue what branding even was when I started. My online presence and community came first, and my brand and blog seamlessly grew from that.

I am so much more than the company or product I represent!

I think that is CRUCIAL to be successful in network marketing.

This would be tip #4. I absolutely adore my company, and could not imagine partnering with another one. But because we don't always have control over what happens with any corporate company, I feel it is wise to **make your brand about MORE than just your business**. Become marketable outside of just the product you represent. After all, that product is only a part of your life; YOU are the real treasure. People follow and join because of YOU and YOUR GIFTS. Your worth and potential are unlimited!

I am a successful person but never pretend to be perfect or even that have it all together.

I run a growing business and have a passion for health and wellness and empowering others. I have found what I'm GOOD at, and I let go of the rest. This is my final tip: **you don't have to be good at it all**, and people actually prefer to see areas in your life that aren't perfect! For example, my brand has nothing to do with organization.

My bed is unmade most days. (Supposedly Sadam Hussein left his bed unmade every day, too . . .)

The fitted sheet on my unmade bed has pen marks all over it from a budding artist.

I only do "do it yourself" projects if I HAVE to.

I don't have a closet full of amazing outfits, and I sure don't have a lot of professional pictures of me in said wardrobe. As a matter of fact, one of my only professional pictures accidentally has my toddler son whizzing in the background! #RealLife

My social media accounts aren't even what I would call "aesthetic."

And guess what? THAT IS MORE THAN OK! So much of my brand comes from me being relatable!

Don't be held to any sort of unrealistic standard, and LET GO OF WHAT DOESN'T RESONATE WITH YOU!

There are so many other influencers who have incredible talents and various niches. We each have our own flair we bring to this world; it's up to you to find what sets you on fire and how you can impact humanity with these gifts.

So share your light with the world. Share boldly, bravely, and genuinely. Make it about more than just YOU—make it about others, and have your brand bring VALUE. Don't worry about it being perfect or excelling at everything. It's actually freeing for not just you but for your audience as well when you allow everyone to be who they are created to be. The power that comes from letting go of the unrealistic and unattainable pressure to be liked by everyone or be perfect at everything is an invitation for other people to be authentic and true as well. There are few things in life that are more precious than helping someone else find their spark.

It is in this way we create lasting change in the world, one spark at a time.

MOMENTUM MAKERS

1. **BE AUTHENTIC. BE YOU.** Find your passion and build your brand around it! The act of sharing genuinely will be the key to your success!
2. **FIND SOMETHING UNIQUE ABOUT YOURSELF OR YOUR FAMILY AND GET GOOD AT SHARING IT.** I find it incredibly inspiring that there are SO MANY successful people in this business, and they each have their own unique gifts.
3. **CARE ABOUT PEOPLE!** The more I cared about my fellow man and their well-being the more my business flourished. People knew I was a safe space. When you find a niche that adds value to the lives of others, loyalty usually follows.
4. **MAKE YOUR BRAND ABOUT MORE THAN JUST YOUR BUSINESS.** Become marketable outside of just the product you represent. After all, that product is only a part of your life, YOU are the real treasure. People follow and join because of YOU and YOUR GIFTS. Your worth and potential are unlimited!
5. **YOU DON'T HAVE TO BE GOOD AT IT ALL, AND PEOPLE ACTUALLY PREFER TO SEE AREAS IN YOUR LIFE THAT AREN'T PERFECT!** For example, my brand has nothing to do with organization. Don't be held to any sort of unrealistic standard and LET GO OF WHAT DOESN'T RESONATE WITH YOU!

CAROLLYN MUSHRO

LEARN YOURSELF, LOVE YOUR LEGACY

"If you're always trying to be normal, you'll never know how amazing you can be."

—Maya Angelou

For most of my life, I felt a sense that I didn't quite belong. In childhood, it started in the classroom, and this feeling carried into high school friend circles. Now, don't get me wrong, I had friends, but I never had that one, constant, can't-live-without-you best friend or crew that I fit into effortlessly. Usually, I was bouncing around from group to group, finding that I identified with the "popular" crowd as much as I did the yearbook editors, as well as the grunge kids I worked with at the music store (remember those relics?). I didn't have a prescribed box or mold that I fit into . . . and I was totally cool with that.

Adulthood was no different . . . I was the girl who traveled the world, studying in foreign countries. Growing up as an only child prepared me well for stepping out on my own and fostering relationships with those I met along the way. As a Spanish major, I learned as much about other cultures as I did myself while partaking in adventures in Costa Rica, Spain & Mexico. I did this without much thought of what was happening back in my homeland (FOMO was still a foreign concept in 2001!).

In motherhood, I was portrayed as the woman who gave birth without medication and breastfed her babies well after they were walking and talking. Our family's food came from a community-supported agriculture group, and our parenting choices were sometimes considered "alternative." In the blue-collar, south suburbs of Chicago, I didn't exactly fit the mold of the traditional parent, yet standing out was nothing new to me. I was steadfast and incredibly confident in who I was and what I stood for. I have always worn my uniqueness on my sleeve like a badge of honor.

Little did I know, my life as an awkward misfit was about to pay off. Literally.

In 2014 I noticed that a friend of mine was sharing on social media about wellness products that were shaping the footprint of her family. I had been exposed to this product at least a handful of times thus far, yet I hadn't encountered that one influential person who made me say yes—YET. Even though this friend was someone I had just virtually "met" in a mom's group on Facebook, energetically, I knew I liked what she stood for. I knew she had high standards for wellness and questioned the status quo like me—a classic case of "like attracts like." This instinctual connection was the magic spark that ignited my "yes." So I reached out to connect with her and enrolled with her in our company. Sight unseen. With only my intuition to guide this divine union!

Soon thereafter, I began casually sharing about these products after witnessing a profound impact on my family. I had an overwhelming response from friends and family who jumped in and wanted to try them. Left and right, it seemed I was enrolling people from every chapter of my life. In my first month, I enrolled 18 people. In my second month, I stopped counting after 20. It was so fast-paced that if a day passed without enrolling someone, I was disappointed. I had NO idea that this was life on easy street as a network marketer. I was clueless!

While I reveled in what seemed to be an "overnight" success out the gate, I also found myself asking how it happened. Some of my colleagues at the time struggled to enroll members, which left me wondering why so many people were willing to say yes to me. Now, I would expect a massive enrollment onboarding from someone with a tight-knit network of friends and a large family, but I had neither of those things. In fact, I was an only child with only six first-cousins on both sides of my family combined! HOW was this even possible for someone like me?!?

It took me months, if not years, to discover why I exploded onto the scene of a business model I knew nothing about. My only formal training to date was in teaching high school Spanish—I didn't have an ounce of "sales" skills in my veins. Somehow, though, I landed amongst those who were unconsciously skilled in this profession. For the time being.

At the time, I was utterly blindsided by the fact that I had been building a personal brand for myself for years prior to discovering my company. The girl who refused to be bound by the status quo had found a company that aligned seamlessly with her alternative viewpoints surrounding natural products, wellness, and bodily autonomy. These two worlds collided, and magic happened!

In retrospect, I was able to discern that I had already established a tribe of trusting followers based on the "alternative" chemical-conscious lifestyle that I led. Families were starting to catch onto the idea of a low-tox lifestyle, and they saw me as a resource in this realm. After all, I wasn't quiet about my viewpoints. I would post on social media every time I saw a news article about natural birth, GMO-foods, or making your own baby wipes. For years I had been establishing a personal brand, albeit unknowingly.

My brand was someone who was unique and unafraid to be herself and stand up for her beliefs. It was someone who adamantly questioned the mainstream narrative. It was someone who wanted to serve as a connector for families looking for wellness options to take charge of their health.

So just like I had inadvertently constructed a brand for myself just by being myself, YOU have one, too! This is different from corporate branding—we aren't talking about a catchy logo or color themes here. I'm talking about your ethos in life—the things you stand for and the ideas your peer group would associate with you.

Have you ever been told, "I read an article the other day and it made me think of you!" Or maybe you receive the perfect gifts for every holiday because everyone in your circle knows your affinity for owls, cross-country skiing, or photography! All of these seemingly random characteristics make up the beautiful, distinctive brand of you.

In the world of network marketing, the ultimate question is "How can I leverage the brand of me in an effort to connect with others?" After all, connection is what it's all about in this biz because in this industry your network represents your net worth. As a result, it literally pays to be cognizant of the brand you're creating for yourself so you can be mindful of the types of people you're attracting to your business! Think of it this way: we watch, measure, track, and even scrutinize our organization's growth on paper . . . let's be intentional about the process of learning and growing ourselves as well!

How can we break this down into steps to make this applicable to our businesses? What if you have NO CLUE what your brand is? Let's break down some steps so you can learn it, love it and even lift it up a notch!

When we connect with others via commonalities—or even characteristics that others WISH to see in themselves—this is called attraction marketing. To put it simply: your vibe will attract your tribe! If your outlook on life is in sync with that of another person, you will both, unconsciously, determine if your ideologies are an energetic match. Remember that I enrolled with my sponsor simply based on a keen awareness that we shared similar values? My very own enrollment process was a perfect example of attraction marketing in action!

1. LEARN IT!

The first step is simply to LEARN yourself. It's essential that you base this process on an understanding of who you are and what makes you tick. One way to hone in on your exclusive characteristics is to create a list of 20, 30, or more words that resonate with your identity. These words can be descriptive adjectives, action verbs, or nouns. I've seen words like "boy mom," abstract concepts like "harmony," and even imagery like "watercolors" on these curated lists. There are no right or wrong words as long as they depict your persona or one you aspire to. What do you want others to think of when they hear your name? Ask your close friends or spouse to help you in this process. It's important that the person lending his or her thoughts is a trusted confidant, not someone who will criticize. An outsider contribution from someone who knows you quite well can offer an honest and open perspective.

After you have a solid list, pare down your words and phrases so you only have about 10 that resonate the most with you. Copy your list proudly into your phone notes. Pen it on pretty paper and keep it next to your workspace. Write it on your bathroom mirror with Expo markers so you can see your chosen words alongside your gorgeous face! Not only will composing this list give you a wonderful exercise in learning yourself, but it will also aid in your awareness of the niche of prospects you are attracting.

2. LOVE IT!

The second step is to LOVE IT! There is nothing more attractive than someone who is confident in his or her own skin. A self-assured person will draw others in like a magnet, no matter your personal brand. If you can master the art of knowing and loving yourself, your confidence will exude in nearly every circumstance.

3. LIFT IT!

Finally, the last step is to LIFT your brand! Your brand can only take you as far as you're willing to grow yourself. The art of knowing and elevating yourself is not only beneficial to your business, but it will also spill out into relationships in your personal life. After all, what holds you back in life will also hold you back in your business, which is why it's imperative to continually invest in your personal growth plan. Think of this as if it were the "background music" to your business. It's a constant, fluid process that will give you an incredible edge if applied consistently.

There are endless ways to grow yourself, which makes the process as personal and unique as your brand itself. Books from authors like Tony Robbins, Gabrielle Bernstein, John D. Maxwell, and Jim Rohn are affordable ways to tap into some of the most influential thought leaders of our time. Personally, I am a huge fan of the Audible app. Listening to books is the secret sauce that allows me to fill the down moments of my day with growth opportunities. I listen while I drive, do dishes, or fold laundry. Journaling, as well as engaging in self-development conferences, and group coaching sessions are a few other ways to improve upon yourself.

This continual growth process is just as essential to your business as enrolling new members. I've personally had success confronting fears, blockers, and excuses while working 1-1 with a life coach once I entered the higher ranks of my company. I knew that cultivating an abundant mindset was something that would serve me time and time again. In fact, I would consider my investments in this arena to be some of the best money I have ever spent! Not only did my incredible coach help me grow my organization, but she also walked me through leaving a more traditional career that was no longer serving me. I was able to say goodbye to my J.O.B. (Just Over Broke) thanks to knowing and growing myself through network marketing.

There will inevitably be peaks and valleys on your business adventure. Elevating your personal brand in this way gives you the tools needed to conquer nearly any obstacle in your path.

No matter where you are on this journey—if you're just starting out or you've been in network marketing for a while now—your personal brand will determine your future trajectory. Knowing and growing yourself will always pay off, yet not always in the ways you would expect. Consider how your hallmark will imprint upon the hearts of the hundreds or thousands who will one day join your organization. The way in which you carry yourself and live out your life has the power to bring change to the world, and your legacy will remain long after you're gone. Your opportunity to craft it begins today!

MOMENTUM MAKERS

1. **LEARN IT!** One way to hone in on your exclusive characteristics is to create a list of 20, 30, or more words that resonate with your identity. There are no right or wrong words as long as they depict your persona or one you aspire to. What do you want others to think of when they hear your name? Pare down your words and phrases so you only have about 10 that resonate the most with you. Write it down everywhere! Not only will composing this list give you a wonderful exercise in learning yourself, but it will also aid in your awareness of the niche of prospects you are attracting.

2. **LOVE IT!** There is nothing more attractive than someone who is confident in his or her own skin. A self-assured person will draw others in like a magnet, no matter your personal brand. If you can master the art of knowing and loving yourself, your confidence will exude in nearly every circumstance.

3. **LIFT YOUR BRAND!** Your brand can only take you as far as you're willing to grow yourself. There are endless ways to grow yourself, which makes the process as personal and unique as your brand itself. Investments in this arena will be some of the best money you ever spend!

SUMMER MEYER

GROWING YOUR BUSINESS & EXPANDING YOUR BRAND AUTHENTICALLY

Two years ago I had zero desire to step foot into the network marketing arena. I had been hit up enough that the thought of being "one of those people" made my skin crawl. But what I did have was a burning desire to help people and a sincere passion for connecting with people. Little did I know, I was building my brand for many years before I became open to network marketing.

I have been in the fitness industry teaching group fitness for the past 20 years, so health and wellness have been a large part of who I am for the majority of my life. I am a mother to four amazing kiddos who keep me full of love and on the brink of insanity most days. Two of our four beautiful children came to us through foster care and adoption. We also openly shared about our infertility struggles, our road to adoption, and most recently my BRCA1 diagnosis and subsequent mastectomy.

I'm sure you're wondering what any of this has to do with you and network marketing. What I will say, being very, very honest, is that it has everything to do with my rapid success. I get asked frequently how I earned six figures in the first year of being in network marketing. First of all, I was blessed with an amazing mentor. I will never ever discount that—it's part of why I wanted to be a part of this book. When I reflect on why my growth was so fast, I have no choice but to look back and realize that I had built a brand for years before jumping in.

Anyone who knows my family, whether on social media or in person, sees that fitness and nutrition are important parts of our lives. I openly share about our struggles and how health is at the forefront of our priorities. Whether it was recovering from surgery or eliminating food coloring from my children's diets to help with focus and behavior, we are an open book.

When we found a line of nutrition supplements we loved (my husband shed 30 lbs. and my energy went through the roof), sharing it was easier than I had ever anticipated because it aligned with who we are. People knew we loved good ingredients and cared deeply about what went into our bodies, so as we began to share about our new business, people already knew it as an area about which we were knowledgeable.

This leads to one of my BIGGEST pieces of advice in regards to branding: make sure the company you are with aligns with YOUR passions. People had witnessed for years my family's commitment to nutrition and overall wellness. Whether it was Facebook posts searching for non-GMO granola bars or exercise tips for the whole family, our network knew we were invested in this area. For example, a stay-at-home mom who decides to sell expensive business suits may have an uphill climb gaining credibility in her brand because, let's face it, she probably isn't wearing many designer suits daily. Another mom who posts frequently on social media about fashion who previously worked at Nordstrom's may have an easier go selling those expensive suits. A bald man selling hair care products might also be a tougher job. NOTHING IS IMPOSSIBLE, but your brand will come together and flow more easily if it's an area you can speak easily to. **So finding a company and products that align with your passions or you've had an incredible product experience with will help you build your brand more quickly.**

Do you have amazing before and after photos? That will help people trust your story and further your brand. Your personal experience is what people trust, especially if they have come to like and follow you. My husband's before and after photos allowed people to see why we were in love with these products, and they knew we already were passionate about quality nutrition and supplements.

Photos of my life and family are on all of my social media pages, which allow people to get to know me and my family outside of just my business. They see us in our daily lives, allowing my humanity to come through. If you are using social media to help grow your business, remember you are your brand, so allow your future customers a peek into what makes you tick. If you are sharing how much more energy you have because of your amazing products, let your friends see you doing things with that energy.

When it comes to branding, get crystal clear on your target market. Who are your best customers? What audience will respond the best to you? Whether it's on social media or in person, knowing the people you want to attract will allow you to grow your brand.

I'm a stay-at-home mom/fitness instructor with four young, busy, and athletic kids. Those are my people. You tend to attract people who are similar to yourself. Many of the people that join my team have very similar interests or struggles. I can speak easily to people about needing quick healthy meals because in a family of six, the struggle is daily, and it resonates with my audience.

It's easiest for me to market and brand with what I know, so when I write a Facebook post, it's with busy, tired moms in mind. When I look for business builders, I look for moms who want to do more for their families because that was me. My very wise mentor, Jessica Reigner, told me when I was beginning to build my business to **find my avatar**. She was exactly right. If you don't get specific on whom you are looking for or what your brand is about, it's too general and won't appeal to anyone. **Find the**

people who relate to your struggles and your dreams. Those are your people.

It's easier for me to get crystal clear on whom I want to help and how I can help when I sit down and think about their needs and how to address those needs. There are millions of people in the world looking for solutions, and when you are able to specifically talk to them about what's hard in their lives, they are more likely to join you as either customers or business builders. I have built my brand around helping tired moms and dads lose inflammation and gain energy so they can enjoy their lives more. Exhausted moms living on leftover mac and cheese who are frustrated that their jeans don't fit, yet are too tired all the time to go to the gym—those are my people. It's who I have built my brand talking to. That's who I write to in my social media posts and who I relate with most in person. So who is your target market?

What makes network marketing so special is it's about connecting. There are not billboards pointing people in a direction of a shop. We are the billboards. It's being authentic and showing up every day.

It's no secret that people buy from people they KNOW, LIKE, and TRUST, so your brand should build those areas. If your content is all about products or sales, your network never gets to know the real you. It's hard to like someone you don't know anything about, and even harder to trust that person.

Your brand is how you show up in the world. You and your energy are the most important aspects of building your brand. No one wants to join a team with someone who is always complaining or posting polarizing things on social media. Be your own billboard. People want to do what you're doing because you look happy and healthy and exude confidence. Good energy attracts good energy, so be the person that people like and trust.

It goes without saying that people will be watching you. Your actions speak louder than words. If you represent a health and wellness company yet show up around town carrying your sugary soda, your credibility might not be great with those who see you. The same goes if you sell nail polish and your nails are never done. Branding is all of it.

I have started pouring into social media. And by pouring in, I mean spreading all kinds of compliments on others' posts. I make genuine comments on the things my friends are sharing with the world. It's helped me reconnect with so many people and has opened up conversations. It has also improved my Facebook algorithm. Facebook will then show them more of my posts, so it's a win all the way around.

Being the person they know, like, and trust by adding value to their lives will take your brand and business to the top of their list when they need something. Plus it feels really good to pour goodness into the world.

MOMENTUM MAKERS

1. **MAKE SURE YOUR COMPANY ALIGNS WITH YOUR PASSION.** Finding a company and products that align with your passions or that you've had an incredible product experience with will help you build your brand quickly.
2. **DOCUMENT YOUR JOURNEY.** Show the "why" to your passion. That will help people trust your story and further your brand. Your personal experience is what people trust, especially if they have come to trust you.
3. **LIST OUT YOUR TARGET MARKET.** If you don't get specific on who you are looking for or what your brand is about, it's too general and won't appeal to anyone. Find the people who relate to your struggles and your dreams. Make sure your brand speaks to them specifically.
4. **BE YOUR BRAND.** Show up in the world as someone people want to be around and your target market will find you. You and your energy are the most important aspects of building your brand. No one wants to join a team with someone who is always complaining or posts polarizing things on social media. Be your own billboard.

COURTNEY LUPER

YOUR SUPERPOWER IS YOU!

The thing I love about social media is it's a place where you can be whoever you want to be. Most people know me as Courtney Luper, "the girl with one million followers" and assume that I have always been this bubbly, outgoing, sparkly, crazy girl who lives life on her own terms. In reality, though my journey started the exact opposite.

I grew up in a small town in Texas—a really small town, like my whole high school was 200-kids-small. Everyone knew everyone, and I was the shy, nerdy girl who always had my face in a book. This was the kind of town where all your neighbors were your relatives; for example, on my block was our family with my mom and dad and siblings, my granny and papa lived next door, my cousins lived behind us, and my grandma and grandpa lived across the street. I thought we owned the block. My favorite memories were going to my granny's house after school. We would watch Oprah, and I thought to myself, "I want to help people the way Oprah does."

Why am I bringing up Oprah, and what does she have to do with branding yourself and building a business online? During the 80s and 90s, talk shows were the rave. They were the way people consumed media just like Facebook, Instagram, and YouTube are today. You could peek into other peoples' lives, and whoever had the best ratings was the most successful talk show. Oprah, without a doubt, dominated not only because of her content but also because of the way she made people feel. Oprah's number one concern was the value she provided and the community she was building with her audience, so when I started consciously building my

Facebook page, I thought to myself, "I want to be like Oprah," and decided my job was to make people feel good when they came to my page—to be the sunshine in their day.

Making people smile is my brand. Really, it is . . . that awkward, small-town girl dreamed big and dreamed of the day when she could live a big life. So what did I do to show that? I brought people into my world without fear of what they would think, from live cooking shows with lots of bloopers to birthday parties, to dressing up in unicorn costumes and going to Walmart with Papa and my friends. I even got married on a live video to one of my followers! I decided it was my job to bring people joy through my experiences.

The problem I see online is so many people haven't decided what their online purpose is. So what do people do when they don't know their purpose? They copy others who are having success. I see it every day—people literally copying others' posts word for word with absolutely zero originality. If building a brand is supposed to be based on you and your interests, how is doing this serving you? How is someone supposed to buy into or connect with you when you don't even know who you are? How does this look to other people? Think of yourself watching TV and changing the channel and every single channel flip is the exact same thing. That's what it looks like when you are copying the big leader on social media because, guess what? A bunch of other people are copying them, too.

The next mistake I see in branding on social media is too many people are chasing the validation checkmark over providing value on their own life and experiences. Because social media branding has become a thing over the last decade as a way to provide extra or full-time income, people are in too much of a rush to try to find something that "works" before finding their unique voice and what works for them. What we have in ourselves is a gift, ourselves, and how we are giving that to the world is a special gift because there is no one like you. Why are you trying to be a copy of somebody else instead of an original?

The last problem I see others make when trying to build a brand is worrying about what other people think. When I first started, I had a lifelong friend block me, and that had me questioning what I was doing online. When I stopped to think about it, what I realized is that losing one friend online was okay. That person wasn't meant for me. Their leaving made space for people who did want to hear me. It's okay because everyone is not meant for us.

So how do you solve all these problems? How do you show up as yourself to actually be a persona that people will associate with or recognize as a real-life brand?

Step One: **Decide who you are and who you want to serve.** Who do you want to speak to? Most of the time you are speaking to those who are past versions of you and sharing how to get to where you are. The people with the following and interaction you want to emulate are doing just that. They aren't trying to be someone else. So grab your notebook and ask yourself these questions. Who am I? What expertise do I have that I can share with others? What do I like to do? What things do I like to buy? What activities bring me joy? What's important to me in life? Don't be afraid to go all out in this journaling process. The more you know, the more clearly you can be on the next parts of this plan. And the more specific you can be brings more clarity, which is better for building a brand. Once you identify what makes you unique, where are you going? What are your hopes and dreams? What are the experiences you want to have? What journey are you on? The more you speak this out loud, the more you speak this into existence and even share this on social media, the more real this becomes.

Funny story for y'all—at the beginning of my social media career, part of my brand was being a single girl on the quest to find my true love, my husband. I am not kidding. I would share with my audience how I really wanted to meet my special someone. As I got to know myself more, one day in 2018, I declared in that year I would be living at the beach and in a serious relationship. I met my husband just a few days afterwards, and he lived 20 minutes from the beach! Now, I am not saying things will happen as quickly for you, but the lesson is that I always post about where I am going, and then it happens.

Let's get back to the first part of what makes you unique! After you journal about your interests, your value, and things you want to learn, GO JOIN GROUPS to make friends with people interested in the same things and PROVIDE VALUE on those things. Do you like to cook? Then go add recipes in the groups and people will add you! Do you like to wear makeup? Go do the same thing in those groups. Give more and you will receive. Find your tribe! If Facebook isn't your jam, then go look up hashtags on Instagram. Post on those things! Make friends! Social media is meant to be SOCIAL, right?

Now, remember that your page is your OWN TV SHOW, so make it like a TV SHOW. Bring people into your world—the ups, downs, and even the challenges! Go live without fear of what you say or how you look. In the beginning, you are going to suck, but keep going and don't give up. Most people give up right before success shows up. My best videos are the ones with the most bloopers. People love to laugh! Laugh at yourself with them! Bring them joy! Next, share all YOUR original content on your main page. People come to your page for YOU, not your leader or another social media star.

This one is huge: the fear of what others think! So many people say to me, "Can I start a new Facebook page to build my business?" My answer is always, "ABSOLUTELY NOT!" You already have trust with people on your personal page, so guess what? Those people are going to be excited for you and curious about the changes you are about to experience. This also means they will be reacting to and sharing your posts! Also in branding yourself, you should only be touching on your products once a week. Just because you join a business doesn't mean your page needs to become an infomercial. Many people think it does, so that's why they want to start their own page. You are not selling; you are sharing and seeing who is interested. Curiosity posts reach a lot more over time than sales posts.

Most people fear being mocked or judged on social media. They are afraid someone is going to say something bad about them, so I have a hard truth: anyone who is successful will have some haters because people are jealous. People are jealous that you have the courage to show up and live your life outside your comfort zone because that's what they wish they had the strength to do. You will never be criticized by someone who is doing more than you. Read that again. Over the years as I have been building my brand, I have discovered that a lot of my haters are hurt or are broken inside. One of my most hurtful haters was a woman who had lost both parents the month before. So I often remind myself that hurting people hurt people. I choose to live by my granny's motto, "Kill 'em with kindness" and I encourage you to do the same.

I understand that the word "branding" can seem intimidating. Social media is flooded with influencers, and you are trying to find where you fit in, but what is so amazing is there is always room for more online. What is even more amazing, though, is that there is only one you. That is your superpower. Embrace that and sparkle on!

MOMENTUM MAKERS

1. **DO LIVE VIDEOS.** This is one great way for people to connect with you. Bring them into your life and world. This means bringing them into your family. Show your spouse, kids, parents, pets, etc. This is going to build relationships and loyalty beyond just the product you are promoting. Feel the fear and do it anyway. Embrace your imperfect self and people will love and respect you more for it.

2. **JOIN GROUPS AND MAKE FRIENDS.** Even if the friends you make aren't interested in your product, you don't know whom they are friends with. Plus they will support your videos and posts, which make you look more credible to people you are sharing with. (NEVER post your business links in anyone's group but your own because that's a way to get blocked quickly!)

3. **DON'T BE AN INFOMERCIAL.** You are not your company. People are NOT following you for your company; they are following YOU for YOU! Your profile needs to have more of YOU and YOUR life than your product. Do NOT post "Join Me". Do NOT post other people's testimonies on your page. Do NOT post your link on your page. Curiosity posts are better and get lots more interaction! Have the sales conversations in messenger.

4. **MAKE YOUR PROFILE YOUR PERSONAL BLOG.** Share your personal story and take them on your journey. Be excited! People love enthusiasm! Get them involved. Bring them into your world!

5. **MAKE GENUINE CONNECTIONS.** Love on people. Go to their pages and respond to their posts. Message them happy birthday! Satisfied customers go away; loving fans stay!

DR. DANA MCGRADY

MAGNETIC BRANDING

Let me start by introducing myself: I'm Dr. Dana McGrady, a holistic DOM (Doctor of Oriental Medicine) with two clinical locations in Florida. I am a mama to three super fun kiddos and am all about family, time freedom, travel, and helping entrepreneurs step into their true authentic power by finding their creative genius. I have a super fun team in network marketing and am always looking to improve, grow, and level up. My book, *Magnetic Soulpreneur*, is all about how to build your network marketing business with heart and soul. If you feel like that's the only way you want to build your business, true to you and with all heart, then you're in the right place. Keep reading, take some notes, and remember, I truly believe that the time is NOW for all of us to make this profession our own.

In the beginning, I really struggled with my social media and my branding. Everything about it was hard for me. I wasn't even active on Facebook until I found our amazing profession. Once I started actively building my network marketing business, found soul friendships with my team leaders, failed a whole lot, and eventually fell in love with the art of network marketing, THAT, my friends, is when I realized that I needed to start branding myself on social media.

I believe that your social media profile is your glorified business card. Let's be real, most people don't keep or use business cards anymore—they simply get the person's name and send a friend request. BING! That perfect stranger will now turn into a friend at the click of a button. He or she will soon know what you ate for dinner last night, what your littlest one's favorite movie is, plus who your best friends and family members are. MORE than that, they will know in a 10-second span whether they would ever do business with you. I know, harsh, sis. I get it. We humans can be judgmental in our minds, but when we glance at someone's social media, we know what their main messages are, what kind of impact they want to make, where their priorities in life are, and how they feel about themselves. We know if they are a positive person or negative and how they see the world. Now just imagine this: after a little focus and a few quality steps daily toward branding yourself with your unique magnetic vibes, a prospect will be able to go to your social media FB profile, hit the follow button, and glance at your story (it's open for the public to see). Suddenly he or she will get drawn in, intrigued by your messaging, your authentic daily portrayal of how it is like on a daily basis, working from home, having three kids, and actively building your network marketing business in a major growth phase. That prospect will now feel like he or she knows, likes and trusts you, and will also feel like they have a window into your life. They will be able to relate to you, and NOW they will want to be a part of your world.

This, my friends, is the art of magnetic branding, the art of ATTRACTION branding. This art form, when you truly implement it on a daily basis, will transform your credibility and will attract higher caliber entrepreneurs to your organization. It will raise the bar for your business and allow you to truly get traction in your business on a grander scale. I am here to help shorten your learning curve. If you follow my proven techniques and implement these strategies, you will quickly be on your way to freedom income, using the art of magnetic branding. Let's get started!

Now, my friends, is the time to get into the nitty-gritty. Pick three to five things that you want people to think of when they come to your social media profile. For example, mine are: Health & Wellness, Mom/Family, Travel/Lifestyle Freedom, Network Marketing Leader, Female Empowerment. I want you to think of having a five-point STAR and you're outlining what each tip of the star means. Do this so that A) you attract the right entrepreneurs to your network and B) they feel like they know, love, and trust you right away. People always do business and purchase from those with whom they feel an emotional connection. We want to make them FEEL and then ultimately ACT on it. We live in an energetic world, and you want the right caliber of entrepreneurs to be energetically drawn to your business. Branding makes that process so much easier. What are your 3-5? Write them down and start using them constantly in your posts and stories.

Ok, now I want you to think of your IDEAL team member. This is a chance for you to design your future leadership team and attract those exact people to your network marketing team. I've done this many, many times in my career. You learn lessons over and over in this profession. This was one of the major learning curves for me. At one point, I realized that I was accepting team members who were full of negativity and drama just because I was so eager to grow my team quickly. Has that ever happened to you? You get so excited that someone says YES to your opportunity that you start working with someone who completely drains your energy and dulls your light. Don't make this mistake, my friends. Decide to do things differently.

I made a decision to attract a different kind of entrepreneur going forward and have a strict no-negativity policy on my team. That decision ultimately helped me to level up. In the year after that, I started attracting entrepreneurs who were my exact avatar: positive, coachable, willing to show up and put in the work, motivated, hard-working, funny, and kind humans. This brought my joy and excitement back for this profession. Working with the right kind of people DOES matter, and you CAN design a life and business that you love using these strategies. Let the law of attraction work for you in all aspects of your life but definitely when choosing who to work with in your network marketing business.

You are in the driver's seat, so you get to decide from the beginning the kind of energetic feel you want on your team. I wanted my team vibes to be elevated. I wanted my team FB group and ZOOMs to be safe havens away from all of the stresses of the world, places for my team members to grow, to feel safe to struggle, to feel supported, to learn, to feel seen & heard, and ultimately have the community support to evolve into the beautiful entrepreneur they are meant to be. I wanted to protect that energy by trying my hardest not to attract any negative, cynical people who would shift that energy. You can decide the same, and I encourage you to do so. Your future team will thank you, and they will stay by your side for the long haul if so.

My next tip is to be UNFORGETTABLE in your branding. Make sure they SEE you, HEAR you, and don't FORGET you! "How do I do this?" you may be asking. "Dr. Dana, I can barely get them to message me back; how am I going to attract them to me and stand out?" I get that question all of the time. The answer is to: Make them FEEL, Make them THINK, Make them LAUGH, and Give them incredible VALUE. Overdeliver on free content and free value, teach them things they haven't thought of before, and make them want to become the best version of themselves and they will never forget you. Every single human has an invisible sign around his or her neck that says, "Make me feel special." If you live by this and make everyone around you authentically feel seen, heard, and important, they will always want to be in your space. Love your team hard and they will never leave. This also goes for all of the people in your social media network. As they are being attracted to your profile, love all over them. People need this more than ever in the world today, and you can be the light that people need to see.

SHOW up consistently as well. If you are there one day and gone the next, you will lose people in your network. Show up authentically and vulnerably. You don't always have to be at your highest and best. That's not normal. You want to be relatable at the same time as showing up consistently in your branding. Weaving the same message through your posts, making people feel something, and asking for engagement will help people have a voice.

I heard something once that really stuck with me. A mentor told me, "Dana, people can be intimidated by you. You will need to reach out to some people and let them know boldly that you are impressed by them and want to work with them." That really made me think. When you talk to someone on the phone, it makes you human and real. Showing up as your true self to your prospects is key. Utilizing voice messages, video messages, and trying to move your convo to a ZOOM or phone call as quickly as possible will always work the best. We have to humanize the process as quickly as possible when using magnetic branding techniques.

In conclusion, I believe in you! This world needs more light workers, kind humans, and authentic souls who believe in helping to impact more lives through network marketing. Helping people to build a residual income, take their power back, and step up into leadership are my favorite parts of this profession. Branding yourselves is the way to truly attract the right entrepreneurs to your team. It raises your credibility and draws the right kind of prospects to you. This will help you to thrive and truly be unforgettable. I believe in you!

MOMENTUM MAKERS

1. **PICK YOUR TOP 3-5 BRANDING POINTS.** What do you want people to think of when they come to your social media profile or website? Think of having a five-point STAR and you're outlining what each tip of the star means.

2. **DESIGN YOUR IDEAL TEAM MEMBER AND THEN TURN AROUND AND ATTRACT THEM TO YOUR BUSINESS.** Make a decision to attract a different kind of entrepreneur and have a strict no-negativity policy on your team. That decision will ultimately help you to level up.

3. **YOU GET TO CHOOSE THE ENERGETIC VIBE ON YOUR TEAM.** Protect elevated energy by trying not to attract any negative, cynical people who would shift that energy. Your future team will thank you, and they will stay by your side for the long haul if so.

4. **BE UNFORGETTABLE AND BOLD.** Make people FEEL and they will ultimately ACT. Over-deliver on free content and free value, teach them things they haven't thought of before, make them want to become the best version of themselves, and they will never forget you.

5. **MOVE ALL OF YOUR SOCIAL MEDIA CONVERSATIONS OFFLINE TO A PHONE CALL OR ZOOM AS QUICKLY AS POSSIBLE.** When you talk to someone on the phone, it makes you human and real. Showing up as your true self to your prospects is key.

JULIE BURKE

POWERHOUSE BRANDING

What if you could really reach your dreams? What if you could finally turn the corner on a career that sets the path you have always wanted?

If you're considering network marketing, new to network marketing, or even if you have been doing it a long time but not quite reaching the hope you had for it, I am going to tell you EXACTLY how I turned my mature network marketing business into my dream life. The secret to success was building a personal brand. When you start realizing that you are the real product, not what you sell or promote, everything changes.

In just one year, by focusing on building my personal brand, I successfully grew three different six-figure revenue streams outside my network marketing business. I had a booked out coaching business, created and sold digital products, and rose quickly to become a super affiliate. All of that was made possible by developing a personal brand.

I got into network marketing because it provided a stepping-stone into entrepreneurship. I loved the freedom you can obtain from it. As a naturally creative person, I felt that network marketing would give me the opportunity to build income the way that best fit my life, my vision, and myself. So I got started and was able to build a successful business and team but always had the thought in the back of my mind, "What if my company were to shut down tomorrow? What would happen to my lucrative revenue stream?" I was ready to take my business and creativity to the next level. I didn't want to continually throw out on social media a "join my product" campaign. I wanted to focus on how to build online businesses, not just network marketing, but businesses that could help generate multiple income streams.

To do that, I had to become a branding expert—and helping others understand what they were really buying into—me. Over the last five years, I've learned many principles that I could point to that have helped me create a successful brand strategy. Below I'm going to give you my top five; but, they really all boil down to this: before people buy into a product, a company, or a program, they have to buy into YOU. Your personal brand matters so much more than the products that you represent or create.

So how do you create a personal brand?

First, **you must identify your brand**. When you're branding yourself, you need to understand yourself first. What do you want people to feel when they interact with your brand? Branding is really about emotions and how people feel when they connect with you. Early on, I knew that I wanted them to see me as trustworthy, real, and fun when I was connecting with others in person or online. I wanted to make others feel good, comfortable, and inspired—that's my brand.

In early 2016, I was in a masterclass and was challenged to decide who I wanted to be when I was creating my brand. I had a choice to make—I could go the health and wellness direction or the entrepreneurial route. How was I going to show up? I was discovering online branding and lead funnels and had created my first course, "5 Steps to 6 Figures", and it was then that I realized that my core brand was much more aligned with being known as an entrepreneur. Did that mean I couldn't post or talk about health and wellness? No. It just meant that my brand, at its core, was going to be focused on entrepreneurship.

How do you identify your brand? You must first really nail two critical points about yourself:

- "What are my core values?"; and,

- "When people interact with me, how do I want them to feel?"

Once you can answer those questions, you're on your way to identifying your brand.

Your next step is to **identify your target audience**. You must know the type of person you want to partner with. Often we are trying to figure out who we want to *sell* to, but that's the wrong question. Your target audience is who you want to be *in relationship with*—ultimately, who is it that you want to work with/to be a part of your team? What are the qualities of your target audience? What are you looking for in a team member or customer?

Understanding this is as important as identifying your core identity. Take some time to clearly identify who you want to work with. Where are they? What is their pain? What commonalities do you have with them? How can you help them—how can you match your solution to what they need? When you've answered these questions, you will have a better idea of the people you're trying to reach with your personal brand.

When you're talking to everyone, you're really talking to no one. That's the trouble with spamming. I've been spammed, and it's the worst—messages flying into my inbox. It's offensive. If you don't get to know me, how do you know that I'm the right fit for you, your product, or your company?

Just recently, I interacted with someone who was clearly not interested in identifying their brand. This person spammed my inbox with a message saying, "Hope everything is going well." A simple look at my profile would have told this person that I was currently in bed sick with COVID! They didn't care about me enough to take the time to identify whether or not I was the right fit for them. They hadn't identified their target audience—they were just spamming and hoping to get a lead.

Don't do this. Take the time to identify your audience so you know exactly who you want to work with.

Next, make sure you **build your brand story bank**. Stories connect us—they're how you become relatable to others. They are the thing people will remember most. In fact, they will remember what you are trying to teach them because they remember the story. It never works the other way around.

Stories are the most powerful tool that network marketers most often overlook. Everyone has a story—from childhood and how we were raised to our life experiences and how we got started in business. What is your story? What do you want people to know about you, and how can you connect your story to a teachable moment . . . something that will bring value to those you lead?

One thing to remember when sharing your story and bringing people into your life is this: it's OK to be vulnerable, but it's not OK to consistently show up as a "hot mess." That's a tightrope you'll have to learn to walk as you create your brand. People want you to be real and honest and show them yourself through your story. But you have to decide what you will share and how it is helpful to them in what they're trying to do. Share stories that will take people on a journey with you. Be vulnerable and straightforward but identify the teachable moment—how you came out on the other side better than you were before.

When I first got started online, I was my mentor told me that I needed to do videos—I almost puked! Facebook Live was brand new, and I was being encouraged to use it as a powerful way to build my brand. I can remember my first time doing a Facebook Live. I was so nervous that I was constantly clicking my pen, and then it went flying across the room! Instead of trying to play it off, I told those who had shown up that I was nervous because it was my first live video, but I was also so excited about what I had to share with them because I believed in my content. I was straight up with them, and people loved it because I was willing to give it a try and be real. They were afraid too, and my story inspired them.

Another step toward building your personal brand is to **create valuable content**. Content is the glue that connects your brand to your product. What are you passionate about? What do you enjoy? What are the things that you can't wait to talk about? When you connect value to your answers to these questions, you're ready to share with your followers—via video (FB Live, YouTube, Instagram, etc.), blogging, email marketing, courses, and programs. You don't have to be an expert—you just have to be willing to take people along with you as you learn. Create curiosity, and people will come along with you on your journey.

Where do you find valuable content? Start by making a list of the top 10-15 things you get excited to talk about—not your company and product but things you really enjoy and are passionate about. I know what's on my list: showing up and creating content, staying fit in my 40s, the importance of collagen, running an online business, self-care, cycling, my kids, building a brand, traveling, wins on my team, my love of food, creating simple meals, my "fur baby" (Lola), and jalapeño margaritas! What's on your list? Once you have your list, start making a list for each item on the list! My guess is that you're going to create a pretty long list of valuable content that you can share with those who follow you!

What do you do when you're not sure what to talk about? Look at your list, tell your story, and discover relevant content from other places like Google or Facebook groups. You can find content all around you: online forums, blogs, podcasts, Reddit. Look for what others in your audience are talking about and create valuable content around that.

Lastly, when you're building your personal brand, make sure you **establish credibility**. Your brand creates your credibility. Your real brand is defined by what people say about you. You are showing others that you have the ability to help them change their lives, and it's all about how you make them feel. People want to feel heard and seen and want to be inspired. Simplify your message. Don't overcomplicate it—just show up and be YOU. People really don't care what you look like. They care about what you have to say. Just make sure you're building your brand with YOUR voice, not someone else's.

When I got started, I wasn't looking to be an influencer, and I was shocked when I would come off stage from sharing at an event, and people wanted to talk to me and would say things like, "I can't believe I'm talking to you." That all happened because I was being real and had established credibility. I would purposely do a FB Live right after doing yoga as a sweaty mess . . . I was going to build my brand on my terms. You can't look outside yourself to create your brand. You have to be true to yourself.

When building your brand, remember that people want to follow a person, not a product. When you identify your brand and target audience, create your brand story bank, create valuable content, and establish credibility, you're well on your way to building your personal brand.

Remember, become your own definition of amazing! Everything you need is right inside of you, waiting to come out to create a bigger brand, more opportunities, and a greater impact.

Don't ever settle and remember . . . YOU CAN HAVE IT ALL!

MOMENTUM MAKERS

1. **REALIZE THAT YOU ARE THE REAL PRODUCT, NOT WHAT YOU SELL OR PROMOTE.** Before people buy into a product, a company, or a program, they have to buy into YOU. Your personal brand matters so much more than the products that you represent or create.

2. **IDENTIFY YOUR BRAND.** Branding is really about emotions and how people feel when they connect with you. Ask yourself: "What are my core values?" and "When people interact with me, how do I want them to feel?"

3. **IDENTIFY YOUR TARGET AUDIENCE.** Your target audience is NOT who you want to *sell* to, but rather who you want to be *in relationship with*—ultimately, who is it that you want to work with/to be a part of your team? What are the qualities of your target audience? What are you looking for in a team member or customer?

4. **BUILD YOUR BRAND STORY BANK.** Share stories that will take people on a journey with you. Be vulnerable and straightforward but identify the teachable moment—how you came out on the other side better than you were before.

5. **CREATE VALUABLE CONTENT.** You don't have to be an expert—you just have to be willing to take people along with you as you learn. Create curiosity, and people will come along with you on your journey.

6. **ESTABLISH CREDIBILITY.** Your real brand is defined by what people say about you. Simplify your message. Don't overcomplicate it—just show up and be YOU.